Playing
the Game

PRAEGER SERIES IN POLITICAL COMMUNICATION

Robert E. Denton, Jr.
General Editor

Rhetorical Studies of National Political Debates: 1960–1988
Edited by Robert E. Friedenberg

Political Communication in America: Second Edition
Robert E. Denton, Jr., and Gary C. Woodward

Access to the Airwaves: The Networks, the Presidency, and the
"Loyal Opposition"
Joe S. Foote

Listening for a President: A Citizen's Campaign Methodology
Ruth M. Gonchar Brennan and Dan F. Hahn

Attack Politics: Strategy and Defense
Michael Pfau and Henry C. Kenski

Playing the Game

The Presidential Rhetoric of Ronald Reagan

Mary E. Stuckey

New York
Westport, Connecticut
London

Library of Congress Cataloging-in-Publication Data

Stuckey, Mary E.
    Playing the game : the presidential rhetoric of Ronald Reagan /
Mary E. Stuckey.
        p.   cm. — (Praeger series in political communication)
    Includes bibliographical references.
    ISBN 0–275–93413–6 (alk. paper)
    1. Reagan, Ronald—Oratory. 2. Rhetoric—Political aspects—
United States—History—20th century. 3. Communication in
politics—United States—History—20th century. 4. United States—
Politics and government—1981–1989.   I. Title.   II. Series.
E877.2.S79   1990
973.927'092—dc20   89-16208

Library of Congress Catalog Card Number: 89–16208
ISBN: 0–275–93413–6

First published in 1990

Praeger Publishers, One Madison Avenue, New York, NY 10010
A division of Greenwood Press, Inc.

Printed in the United States of America

The paper used in this book complies with the
Permanent Paper Standard issued by the National
Information Standards Organization (Z39.48–1984).

10 9 8 7 6 5 4 3 2 1

This book is dedicated
to my family, especially
Janet, my grandmother,
Steve, my brother, and Pamela, my sister

Contents

Tables

Series Foreword

Those of us from the discipline of communication studies have long believed that communication is prior to all other fields of inquiry. In several other forums I have argued that the essence of politics is "talk" or human interaction.[1] Such interaction may be formal or informal, verbal or nonverbal, public or private, but always persuasive, forcing us consciously or subconsciously to interpret, to evaluate, and to act. Communication is the vehicle for human action.

From this perspective, it is not surprising that Aristotle recognized the natural kinship of politics and communication in his writings of *Politics* and *Rhetoric*. In the former, he establishes that humans are "political beings [who] alone of the animals [are] furnished with the faculty of language."[2] And in the latter, he begins his systematic analysis of discourse by proclaiming that "rhetorical study, in its strict sense, is concerned with the modes of persuasion."[3] Thus, it was recognized over fifteen hundred years ago that politics and communication go hand in hand because they are essential parts of human nature.

Back in 1981, Dan Nimmo and Keith Sanders proclaimed that political communication was an emerging field.[4] Although its origin, as noted, dates back centuries, a "self-consciously cross-disciplinary" focus began in the late 1950s. Thousands of books and articles later, colleges and universities offer a variety of graduate and undergraduate coursework in the area in such diverse departments as communication, mass communication, journalism, political science, and sociology.[5] In Nimmo and Sanders' early assessment, the "key areas of inquiry" included rhetorical analysis, propaganda analysis, attitude change studies, voting studies, government and the news media, functional and systems analyses, technological changes, media technologies, campaign techniques, and research techniques.[6] In a survey of the state of field in 1983 by the same authors and Lynda Kaid, they found additional, more specific areas of concerns such as the presidency, political polls, public opinion, debates, and advertising to name a few.[7] Since the first study, they also noted a shift away from the rather strict behavioral approach.

Then as now, the field of political communication continues to emerge. There is no precise definition, method, or disciplinary home of the area of inquiry. Its domain, quite simply, is the role, processes, and effects of communication within the context of politics.

In 1985, the editors of *Political Communication Yearbook: 1984* noted that "more things are happening in the study, teaching, and practice of political communication than can be captured within the space limitations of the relatively few publications available."[8] In addition, they argued that the backgrounds of "those involved in the field [are] so varied and pluralist in outlook and approach, . . . it [is] a mistake to adhere slavishly to any set format in shaping the content."[9]

The Praeger Series in Political Communication is intended to explore this philosophical stance. The series is open to all qualitative and quantitative methodologies as well as to contemporary and historical studies. The key to characterizing the studies in the series is the focus on communication variables or activities within a political context or dimension.

Mary Stuckey, a political scientist, provides an analysis of the rhetoric of Ronald Reagan. As a companion to an earlier volume focusing on Reagan's rhetoric prior to his election as president, this book investigates how his use of language was instrumental in the creation and maintenance of the "teflon presidency." For Stuckey, rhetoric is the focus of the study not just because of Reagan's communication skill, but also because rhetoric provides a "unique and valuable" insight into the office of the modern presidency.

There are several contributions this book makes to the study of political communication. First, this study makes a detailed and an insightful analysis of the rhetoric of Ronald Reagan. It is a comprehensive study and provides a basis for future specific applications or events of study of the Reagan presidency. Second, the study contributes to our theoretical knowledge of the role and function of rhetoric in the modern presidency. For example, particularly useful is the definition and explication of the notion that effective rhetoric has the two major components of preparation and saturation. Also, in terms of foreign policy, the importance of a president providing an interpretive framework to ensure public understanding and support is well demonstrated: "If a president's greatest asset is his ability to control the agenda and the public interpretation of that agenda, he must speak loudly and often, and whenever possible, he must be the only one speaking authoritatively."[10] Finally, the book provides useful insight and speculation about the nature of the state of rhetoric in the "post-Reagan era."

I am, without shame or modesty, a fan of the series. The joy of serving as its editor is in participating in the dialogue of the field of political communication and in reading the contributors' works. I invite you to join me.

Robert E. Denton, Jr.
Blacksburg, Virginia
1989

NOTES

1. See for example, Robert E. Denton, Jr., *The Symbolic Dimensions of the American Presidency* (Prospect Heights, Ill.: Waveland Press, 1981); Robert E. Denton, Jr., and Gary Woodward, *Political Communication in America* (New York: Praeger, 1985); and Robert E. Denton, Jr., and Dan Hahn, *Presidential Communication* (New York: Praeger, 1986).

2. Aristotle, *The Politics of Aristotle*, trans. Ernest Barker (New York: Oxford University Press, 1970), p. 5.

3. Aristotle, *Rhetoric*, trans. Rhys Roberts (New York: Modern Library, 1954), p. 22.

4. Dan Nimmo and Keith Sanders, "Introduction: The Emergence of Political Communication as a Field," *Handbook of Political Communication*, eds. Dan Nimmo and Keith Sanders (Beverly Hills, Calif.: Sage, 1981), pp. 12–15.

5. Nimmo and Sanders, "Introduction," p. 15.

6. Nimmo and Sanders, "Introduction," pp. 16–27.

7. Keith Sanders, Lynda Kaid, and Dan Nimmo, eds., *Political Communication Yearbook: 1984* (Carbondale, Ill.: Southern Illinois University Press, 1985), p. 284.

8. Sanders et al., *Political Communication*, p. xiv.

9. Sanders et al., *Political Communication*, p. xiv.

10. Chapter 5, p. 90.

Acknowledgments

Many people have contributed to this work, although its faults are mine alone. The writing of this book was partially supported by a summer grant from the University of Mississippi, College of Liberal Arts. Thanks are due to the library staff at the University of Mississippi, particularly Laura Harper at the Government Documents Center and Sharon Schreibner of the Ole Miss Library; to Brian Staley and Ramona Thomas, for their counting, xeroxing, collating, and stapling; and to Ryan Barilleaux, Daniel Geller, Laurie Rhodebeck, and many anonymous reviewers for their criticism and comments. Special thanks are due to Robert E. Denton, Jr., for his kindness and encouragement. I would also like to thank Bill Davisson, John Kennedy, Jr., Lisa Walker, Pallavi Trivedi, John Winkle, and my colleagues at the University of Mississippi for their personal and professional support while this book was being written. Finally, I would like to thank the editors at Praeger, Alison Bricken and Frank Welsch, as well as copy editor Suzanne Ochoa, for their professionalism and skill.

Introduction

This book is intended as a companion volume to *Getting Into the Game: The Pre-Presidential Rhetoric of Ronald Reagan*,[1] which explores Reagan's rise to the presidency through an examination of his public speech prior to his election in 1980. This study is a further exploration of the Reagan rhetoric. Specifically, it is a study of the rhetoric of the "Reagan revolution" and how that rhetoric supported, impeded, and affected Reagan's policy goals and political success. My thesis is that Reagan's use of language in his public speech was instrumental to the creation and maintenance of the "teflon presidency," and that this use of language created a situation whereby the teflon was bound to crack, as it did in 1986. Further, it is my contention that Reagan's rhetorical success was built around foreign policy events, and this is why a foreign policy event (in the shape of Iran/Contra) provided the most conspicuous failure of the Reagan administration.

Rhetoric is the focus of the study for three reasons: first, public speech and public speaking are increasingly important elements in our understanding of the modern presidency; second, Reagan's communicative skill has been an integral part of his presidency; finally, as a methodological focus, the study of rhetoric provides a unique and valuable vantage point from which to view a specific president as well as the office of the presidency.

Rhetoric has become increasingly important to modern presidents, who spend more and more of their time on their public speech.[2] Consequently, scholarly attention is becoming increasingly focused on the nature of the "plebiscitary presidency"[3] and the various strategies involved in "going public."[4] It is becoming increasingly evident that if we are to understand the modern presidency, we must also understand modern presidential rhetoric. As Robert E. Denton and Dan F. Hahn point out, presidential language stimulates and justifies action, and can "inspire, comfort, and motivate the nation . . . [provide] the feeling of a human relationship with our leader . . . encourage justice or injustice . . . their words have encompassed our grief [Lincoln's Gettysburg Address], given us hope [Franklin Roosevelt's first inaugural address], and challenged us to address the task at hand [Kennedy's inaugural]."[5]

Whatever other powers and roles presidents have, it is clear that they function as "interpreters in chief" for the U.S. public. As politics become more and more of a "word game"[6] where "political events . . . are largely creations of the language used to describe them,"[7] the president's role becomes increasingly important. As the focal point of the national government and the representative of the only branch of government able to speak with one voice, the president's interpretation of events often becomes (for better or for worse) the definitive interpretation.[8]

This understanding of politics is supported by the "symbolic interactionist" school of social psychology. Begun by George Herbert Mead and systematized by Herbert Blumer,[9] symbolic interactionism can best be described as a "communication theory of human behavior."[10] Symbolic interactionism is based on the notion that social life is a process during which humans create meaning for themselves through interaction with others. Such interaction is predicated on the use of symbols. For the symbolic interactionist, both individual and group behaviors are based upon the interpretation of key societal symbols. That behavior will in turn affect the reality in which those symbols are embedded, thus altering or reinforcing the existing interpretation.[11] Thus, "for the symbolic interactionist, reality is a social product arising from interaction or communication."[12] In order to understand an individual or a society, therefore, one must understand the relevant symbol system. One does this by examining "roles" on the individual level and "situations" on the societal level.

It is important to note here that neither role nor situation is a static precise element with unalterable rules of pre- or proscribed behavior. The boundaries are socially determined in an ongoing process. "Individuals are constantly interacting, developing, and shaping society. People exist in action and consequently must be viewed in terms of action."[13] This action is both verbal and nonverbal, but language plays a key role as a component of communication.

It is also important to point out that even in democratic societies, all actors are not equal.[14] The president, as a social object, has a different status from that of a citizen, and thus has more influence in terms of socially determined meaning. Given this, it is vital that scholars devote attention to the content of the interpretations that presidents offer as well as to the roles those interpretations play in our national politics and national political culture.

This need is particularly evident with regard to Ronald Reagan's presidency; Reagan understood the communicative nature of the U.S. presidency and used it to his advantage.[15] Despite the criticism that Reagan received as a result of his communications strategy,[16] an awareness of the organizational requirements of the media served Reagan well. Of all the modern presidencies, that of the "Great Communicator" was predominantly grounded in public communication. Reagan and his staff orchestrated his public persona with a tremendous amount of care and attention. As Garry Wills points out, Reagan "is making a public argument, not merely a grand appearance. This is not just a matter of window dressing, but of constant analysis and testing of people's reactions. He is selling substance, not appearance—just as the advertiser is selling the product, not the slogan."[17]

The characteristics of Reagan's rhetoric have been well documented. The most important aspect of that rhetoric is the vision that Reagan projects,[18] a vision that revolves around the parable of "the American dream"[19] and its relationship to the hopes and aspirations of the American public. This gives him the ability to allow Americans to forget the struggles of the present, and focus on "the lost summertime of the nation's past, when neighborhoods were safe, when families held together, when U.S. power bestrode the world."[20]

This vision is supported by metaphoric language,[21] a tendency to divide the world into clear heroes and villains,[22] simplification, cinematic language, themes involving community, and the tendency to treat criticism of himself as criticism of the United States.[23] In addition, Reagan has the gift of presenting his beliefs in simple, emotionally evocative symbolic slogans,[24] delivered in a warm, comforting, and sincere manner.[25]

Reagan has been one of the most ideologically consistent and directive presidents of the modern era, but as Fred I. Greenstein indicates, it is not always easy to turn aphorisms into policy.[26] It is only through a careful and systematic analysis of Reagan's rhetoric, carried out with specific regard to the politics connected to that rhetoric, that we can develop an accurate understanding of the relationship between rhetoric and policy during the Reagan administration.

It is this perspective that makes the focus on rhetoric such a valuable approach, for it is a methodology that unites questions of cultural values, ethical concerns, and policy outcomes.[27] As a methodology, rhetorical analysis takes into consideration the belief that the relationship between politics and political language is a reciprocal one—that the way in which we talk about things is capable of reconstituting the reality in which those things are embedded.[28] The study of rhetoric is thus an inclusive methodology and one that allows the analyst a unique viewpoint into the political world.[29]

Rhetorical analysis is a multidisciplinary approach, drawing from linguistics, anthropology, and philosophy.[30] Its greatest strength, and clearest potential weakness, is that it is interpretive. It is much closer to the philosophical rather than the scientific intellectual tradition. The methodology involves ascertaining answers to certain questions. These questions concern the reasons behind the rhetor's choice of rhetorical strategies, the consistency among and between those strategies, the probable effectiveness of the strategies on supportive and/or opposing audiences, and the context within which the strategies are played out.[31]

Because of its reliance upon interpretive techniques, it is clear that it is neither possible nor desirable for rhetorical analysis to be systematized. It is a technique that is unlikely to be easily or exactly replicated.[32] The analyst is still bound by the rules of evidence, however, and good interpretation will minimize the "personal responses, peculiar tastes, and singularities of the critic."[33]

The goal of rhetorical analysis is to uncover the meaning of a text. That meaning resides in "the life of the reading itself, to which both the text and the reader contribute. . . . What is to be sought among readings of a text . . . is not identity, for there can never be that, but consistency and mutual instructiveness."[34] No interpretation is definitive, for the meaning of a text changes with the context in which it is read. But a good interpretation will offer tools by which we can attain an understanding of both the context within which the text was created and the context within which it is read.

The critic thus walks a precarious line between mechanical and arid analysis of a text according to pseudoscientific rules and arbitrary and capricious interpretation based on personal whim. Both of these extremes can be avoided, however, and rhetorical analysis can provide an enriching and important contribution to our understanding of politics. With this in mind, I invite the reader to share my understanding of the rhetoric of the Reagan presidency, and its relationship to the American political experience.

The data for the study include all speeches, remarks, addresses, statements, memorandums, proclamations, and other forms of public speech of over one page in length during the Reagan presidency.[35] Routine messages to Congress, nominations, and executive orders are excluded. Memorandums and proclamations of under one page in length are also excluded, since their function is deemed largely ceremonial and ceremonial messages reinforce an existing image rather than create a new one. In addition, any effect that these messages have is presumed to be captured by including the longer ceremonial messages. The exclusion of the shorter ones merely removes some of the flotsam without risking anything of substance. All of the data come from the *Public Papers of the President*, published by the Government Printing Office. The documents are cited by title and date. The speeches were given at the White House unless otherwise specified. There are a total of 1,968 documents.

The design of the book is both chronological and thematic, which is possible given the theme of the development of Reagan's rhetoric over time and the eventual exposition of its inherent weaknesses. Chapter 1, "Ronald Reagan and the National Media," is an analysis of Reagan's relationship with the White House press corps. It focuses on the institutional and rhetorical factors that contributed to Reagan's success with the media. Chapter 2, "Revolution: Reagan's First Years," details the first two years of the Reagan presidency, and analyzes the learning process by examining both the smooth and rough spots of those years. Chapter 3, "Consolidation: The Teflon President," focuses on the foreign policy events of 1983–85, and on how Reagan and his staff used those events to consolidate his personal standing. Chapter 4, "Cracks in the Teflon," provides an exegesis of the unraveling of that success between 1986–88, and Reagan's increasing vulnerability to criticism. Chapter 5, "The Great Communicator?," provides a summary of the rhetorical aspects of Reagan's presidency, and discusses lessons from the past and his legacy for the future. The concluding chapter, an epilogue, focuses on Reagan's rhetorical legacy through an examination of the public speech of various candidates from the 1988 presidential election.

NOTES

1. Mary E. Stuckey, *Getting Into the Game: The Pre-Presidential Rhetoric of Ronald Reagan* (New York: Praeger, 1989).

2. James Ceasar et al., "The Rise of the Rhetorical Presidency," *Presidential Studies Quarterly* 11 (Spring 1981): 233–51; Jeffery K. Tulis, *The Rhetorical Presidency* (Princeton: Princeton University Press, 1987).

3. Theodore Lowi, *The Personal President: Power Invested, Promise Unfulfilled* (Ithaca: Cornell University Press, 1985).

4. Samuel Kernell, *Going Public: New Strategies of Presidential Leadership* (Washington, D.C.: CQ Press, 1986).

5. Robert E. Denton and Dan F. Hahn, *Presidential Communication: Description and Analysis* (New York: Praeger, 1986); Walter R. Fisher, "Rhetorical Fiction and the Presidency," *Quarterly Journal of Speech*, Vol. 66, No. 2 (1980): 119–26.

6. Denton and Hahn, *Presidential Communication*, p. 5.

7. Murray Edelman, "Myths, Metaphors, and Political Conformity." *Psychiatry* 30 (1967): 217–28.

8. Lou Cannon, *Reagan* (New York: G. P. Putnam's Sons, 1982), p. 196.

9. Jerome Manis and Bernard Meltzer, eds., *Symbolic Interaction: A Reader in Social Psychology* (Englewood Cliffs, N.J.: Prentice-Hall, 1969).

10. Robert E. Denton, Jr., *The Symbolic Dimensions of the American Presidency* (Prospect Heights, Ill.: Waveland Press, 1981), p. 16.

11. Denton, *Symbolic Dimensions*, p. 21.

12. Denton, *Symbolic Dimensions*, p. 23.

13. Denton, *Symbolic Dimensions*, p. 30.

14. Symbolic interactionism does not take power relations into account, but it is safe to argue that in any social interchange, some actors will have a louder voice than others.

15. Michael Baruch Grossman and Martha Joynt Kumar, "The Limits of Persuasion: Political Communications in the Reagan and Carter Administrations" (Paper delivered at the Annual Meeting of the American Political Science Association, Chicago, Ill., August 1987); Fred I. Greenstein, "Reagan and the Lore of the Modern Presidency: What Have We Learned?," in *The Reagan Presidency: An Early Assessment*, ed. Fred I. Greenstein (Baltimore: Johns Hopkins University Press, 1983), p. 168; Dorothy B. James, "Television and the Syntax of Presidential Leadership," *Presidential Studies Quarterly*, Vol. 18, No. 4 (1988): 737–39.

16. For a summary and historical perspective on this criticism, see John Tebbel and Sarah Miles Watts, *The Press and the Presidency: From George Washington to Ronald Reagan* (New York, Oxford: Oxford University Press, 1985); John Orman, "Reagan's Imperial Presidency" (Paper delivered at the Annual Meeting of the American Political Science Association, Chicago, Ill., August 1987).

17. Garry Wills, *Reagan's America: Innocents at Home* (Garden City, N.Y.: Doubleday, 1985), p. 324.

18. Cannon, *Reagan*, p. 372.

19. Wills, *Reagan's America*, p. 5.

20. Dean Alger, "The Presidency, the Bureaucracy, and the People: Discretion in Implementation and the Source of Legitimacy Question"

(Paper delivered at the annual meeting of the American Political Science Association, New Orleans, La., August 1985), p. 13; Wayne W. Shannon, "Mr. Reagan Goes to Washington: Teaching Exceptional America," *Public Opinion* 4 (December/January 1982): 13–17.

21. Denton and Hahn, *Presidential Communication*, p. 68.

22. Paul D. Erickson, *Reagan Speaks: The Making of an American Myth* (New York: New York University Press, 1985), p. 62.

23. Craig Allen Smith, "Trouble Came to MisteReagan's Neighborhood: Observations on Iran/Contra and the Reagan Rhetoric" (Paper delivered at the Annual Meeting of the American Political Science Association, Washington, D.C., August 1988).

24. Wills, *Reagan's America*, pp. 322–23.

25. David Smith and Melinda Gebble, *Reagan for Beginners* (London: Writers and Readers Publishing Co., 1984), p. 65.

26. Greenstein, "Reagan and the Lore of the Modern Presidency," p. 171.

27. Roderick P. Hart, *Verbal Style and the Presidency: A Computer-Based Analysis* (Orlando, Fla.: Academic Press, 1984), p. 4; James R. Andrews, *The Practice of Rhetorical Criticism* (New York: Macmillan, 1983), p. 24.

28. James Boyd White, *When Words Lose Their Meaning: Constitutions and Reconstitutions of Language, Character, and Community* (Chicago: University of Chicago Press, 1984), p. 4; George Orwell, "Politics and the English Language," in *The Orwell Reader*, ed. George Orwell (New York: Harcourt, Brace, and World, 1956), pp. 355–66.

29. White, *When Words Lose Their Meaning*, p. 280.

30. Denton and Hahn, *Presidential Communication*, p. xii.

31. Theodore Otto Windt, "Presidential Rhetoric: Definition of a Field of Study," *Presidential Studies Quarterly*, Vol. 16, No. 1 (1986): 102–16.

32. Edwin Black, *Rhetorical Criticism: A Study in Method* (Madison: University of Wisconsin Press, 1978), p. xi.

33. Black, *Rhetorical Criticism*, p. 76.

34. White, *When Words Lose Their Meaning*, p. 19.

35. The documents for January 1–20, 1989 are included in 1988.

Chapter 1

Ronald Reagan and the National Media

INTRODUCTION

Perhaps the single best-known feature of the Reagan presidency is his extraordinary success with the U.S. media. Labeled the "Great Communicator" and the "Teflon President," Reagan's reputation as a master of imagery far exceeds his reputation as a master of substance. Hand in hand with this reputation, however, comes criticism of the national media, those cowardly members of the Washington media corps who have somehow "let him get away with it." There is a feeling that if only the media had done their job, the public perception of the Reagan presidency would be very different. Clearly, Reagan's relationship with the national media is an important aspect of his rhetorical success. This chapter presents an analysis of that relationship by examining both the institutional and rhetorical aspects of Reagan's dealing with the White House media corps. It is unlike the other analytic chapters in this volume in that the data are from every year of Reagan's presidency and focus on thematic and tactical concerns, rather than change and development over time.

Ithiel de Sola Pool describes "the whole relationship of reporter and politician" as one that "resembles a bad marriage. They cannot live without each other, nor can they live without hostility.... [I]t is conflict within a shared system."[1] There is widespread agreement by both reporters and officials on the accuracy of that description, particularly as it pertains to a "shared system." There is also agreement in the literature that the rules governing that system have undergone changes in the days since Watergate and Vietnam. Among these changes are an increase in the numbers of the Washington media corps,[2] an increase in cynicism and perceived bias in reporters and reporting,[3] and an increase in the media's access to "the trappings of power," including access to documents, special quarters, and "fantastic amounts of government time and money."[4] It is not a coincidence that all of these changes involve "increases." The national media assigned to Washington are bigger and more powerful than ever before. And along with this power comes a suspicion of both the power and those who wield it. As George Will says, "One thing, at least, is clear. Today the news business is newsworthy. There is almost as much interest in what the press is doing with the news as there is with the news itself."[5]

A brief look at the literature reveals that any president would have certain advantages in dealing with the media in the prevailing political climate. As one author says, "The fact that politicians believe political mileage can be made by venting their long-standing ire with the press is merely a sign that, in the credibility war, the press is not doing too well."[6] This is evident to most observers. What is not evident is why the press is "not doing too well," and why the American people are increasingly doubtful of the media and are more willing to be suspicious of it than the government is.[7]

One answer is that people are simply tired—tired of being lied to by their presidents, tired of feeling abused by those in power, and tired of being told about it by the media. Working on a "kill-the- messenger" philosophy, the feeling seems to be that we would rather disbelieve the messenger than cope with the message.[8] There is a good deal of evidence that whether the American people feel that way or not, the U.S. media believe that they do. The media are "acutely concerned with what *Newsweek* referred to as 'backlash': that they might be accused of inflating their reportage and of feverishly chasing exclusives, propelled by visions of a Pulitzer Prize. . . . [They] studiously tried to avoid [being] vulnerable to charges of shoddy journalism for the sake of personal and professional acclaim."[9] Other authors agree, making statements like, "[The media] cowers in dread of being called 'too powerful.' For the myth of media power, which the media never contested in their salad days, is now being used by the enemies of liberty to incite the people against a free press."[10]

While this is a persuasive argument, it neglects the role of the people in this "incitement." There seems to be a fundamental element in the cultural psyche of the United States that allows this fear of media power. Ronald Reagan is not the first national politician to appeal to this aspect of our psyche: Richard Nixon did it, clumsily; Spiro Agnew did it, vituperatively. Americans are historically suspicious of "bigness" and centralized power.[11] As the 1970s passed into the 1980s, and Americans heard more and more about how the Washington press had toppled a president, the myth of monolithic media power became not only prevalent in the United States, but disturbing as well.[12]

Media power is particularly disturbing to many people when it confronts a popular president. Given Reagan's widespread image of amiability and the astonishing level of personal support he attained, whenever the media challenged him, they were not perceived as pursuing presidential accountability, but as "hounding that poor man."[13]

Like so many other aspects of the presidency, the seeds for the use and abuse of media power were there when Reagan entered the White House, and his techniques for such use and abuse will remain long after he leaves. In order to understand the changes he made in the relationship between the presidency and the press, we must look at how he positioned himself to make such changes possible.

This entire relationship does not, of course, depend upon presidential speech; many other factors are also important. In analyzing the relationship between the president and the media, however, presidential speech has been too often ignored. This study is an attempt to correct that oversight by focusing on presidential speech as a determinant of public perception of the relationship between the president and the national press corps.

RONALD REAGAN'S MEDIA-RELATED
RHETORIC

The data begin on January 20, 1981 and continue through January 20, 1989. The total number of documents relevant to this chapter is 444. Relevant documents include news conferences, "Remarks to Reporters" (with or without question and answer periods),[14] interviews, speeches given to media groups,[15] and "Informal Exchanges with Reporters." This last category is perhaps the most revealing, since it comprises the "helicopter responses": those questions asked as Reagan was on his way to other events, at photo opportunities, and whenever the press could get his attention. They are the shortest documents included, rarely exceeding one-half to a full page (press conferences, on the other hand, averaged six pages in length). A summary of the data is presented in Table 1.1.

One thing is immediately obvious from the table; the number of formal meetings, while quite high in 1981, drops significantly through the rest of his presidency. This reflects the attempts of the Reagan administration to control the president's public image, and bears out the conventional wisdom that Reagan's aides seem to think that the fewer off-the-cuff remarks made by the president, the better.[16]

Other patterns reflect the demands of campaign politics and Reagan's role as "Chief Campaigner" for the Republicans. Both the number of "Interviews with Non-national Media" and those with national media increase during elections and fall off afterwards. Another advantage of the non-national media is that they tend to be more respectful, less aggressive, and more willing to let the president control the agenda and the interview. It is somewhat surprising, then, that Reagan did not return to the non-national media late in this second term, when the Iran/Contra scandal broke. Instead, he and his aides simply reduced access to all media. It is hard to argue with an apparently successful strategy, but it is a surprising one to choose, as it left the president open to charges of evading the press.

Not all questions and answers in each document were included. A series of questions on the same topic were counted

Table 1.1
Ronald Reagan's Speech with the Media

Document	'81	'82	'83	'84	'85	'86	'87	'88	N
News Conferences	6	8	7	5	6	6	4	4	46
Remarks to Reporters	7	3	2	0	4	1	7	0	24
Remarks With Q & A	6	9	13	8	11	7	12	16	82
Formal Q&A With Reporters	3	14	14	21	2	0	0	0	54
Interviews With Nat'l Media	4	1	5	13	9	4	3	3	42
Interviews, Exchanges, Q&A With Non-nat'l Media	2	8	7	10	7	7	2	2	45
Informal Exchanges	18	4	1	5	17	14	29	23	111
Remarks to Media Grps/ Grps About Media	1	6	1	0	1	0	1	4	14
Other	0	1	3	2	0	0	5	15	26
N	47	54	53	64	57	39	63	67	444

as one question. In cases where the media would press for a direct answer, clarification, or specific information, the entire series was counted as one response and classified according to the final result. A clarification was recorded as a direct answer, even if it took ten questions to elicit that answer. A series of questions that resulted in continued deflections, evasions, or nonanswers were also counted as one answer and recorded under the response category that most accurately described the tone of the exchange. All documents included were read and coded three separate times to ensure maximum accuracy and consistency.

The categories for this study reflect the speech patterns of Ronald Reagan regarding the media. They were developed during a preliminary reading of Reagan's rhetoric about the media. Other categories were initially included; those having fewer than ten total entries were either discarded or combined with another category.

There are four main groups of tactics used by Ronald Reagan in his credibility war with the media. The first and most powerful tactic is discrediting his opposition and the media. The second tactic is evasion, which combines delaying, deflection, and direct evasion. The third tactic involves staging, or how the president presents himself to the media and the public. The final tactic is secrecy: how Reagan avoids public debate on—and public knowledge of—certain issues. A summary of Reagan's rhetoric is presented in Table 1.2.

Several things are indicated by this table. In the first place, "Direct Answer" is the single most common response. This is less impressive, however, when we realize that all of the other responses listed are forms of evasion, avoidance, and obfuscation. This realization gives us a very different perspective: instead of Reagan's dominant response being "Direct Answer," it is evasion. In this sample, Reagan used various forms of evasion 3,755 times (80%), and directly answered questions only 960 times (20%). In interpreting this, however, one must remember that not all evasions are unreasonable. All presidents, like all politicians, face questions that they do not want to answer. The media do not always ask questions that need answers or that should be answered, and it would be foolish to assume that they do. Some of the questions asked of the president were therefore dropped. These questions were of the "when did you stop beating your wife?" variety—questions to which there is

Table 1.2
Reagan's Responses to the Media

Response	'81	'82	'83	'84	'85	'86	'87	'88	N
Direct Answers	96	139	110	133	123	105	139	115	960
Delaying: "I don't know" "Further study" etc.	66	102	93	130	137	163	27	79	797
Symbolic	12	70	40	160	164	147	22	25	640
Direct Evasion	48	112	67	91	42	61	17	20	458
Discredits Opposition	6	59	96	154	65	61	5	19	465
Blames Media	7	84	70	40	91	67	20	11	390
Non-answer	49	33	49	120	60	24	5	46	386
Historical/ Personal Evasion	23	52	51	73	42	21	13	19	294
Refers/Cites Others	42	50	12	34	9	7	6	11	171
Deflections: Humor/Story/ Anecdote	4	3	19	56	37	12	10	13	154
N	353	704	607	991	770	668	264	358	4715

no unincriminating answer. Examples include: "When will you admit how much you knew about the arms-for-hostages deal?," and "Is the subway murderer guilty?," which was asked while the case was still before a jury.

Discrediting the Opposition and the Media

Despite the reasonableness of evading questions—and all reasonable questions were included ("How much did you know about arms for hostages?" would not be thrown out)—Reagan still has a variety of ways and means of avoiding questions. The first tactic Reagan employs is the technique of discrediting his opposition. Reagan seizes the moral high ground and leaves his opponents in a defensive and rhetorically weak position. This is even more effective, of course, when the opposition is not present at the time of the accusations. Reagan has three tactics for discrediting the opposition: they are politically motivated, seeking to drag the dirt of politics into an issue that should be clear of any such taint;[17] they are flat out liars and cannot be trusted;[18] or they are petty examples of a lower form of life and can be safely ignored.[19]

All of these responses, and others like them, are quotable, tidy, and emotionally satisfying. They do not, however, reveal much of the substance of the debate. What they do achieve is to structure the debate in emotional and symbolic terms. Reagan's opposition is placed on the "wrong" side of the issue; anyone who disagrees with him becomes unpatriotic at best and treasonous at worst. And, in fact, nearly all of the responses aimed at discrediting his opposition come in concert with symbolic stances (400 out of the 465, or 86%).[20]

This tactic, in all of its forms, functions to influence public opinion of the president's opposition. Since the president has the loudest voice in U.S. politics, those opposing his policies or positions are placed in a position that is, by definition, defensive if the president's interpretation is accepted. Before they can proceed with their arguments, they must first prove to the public that they are not motivated by politics, but by the national interest, and that they can be trusted and are worthy of notice.[21]

This is particularly difficult to accomplish when the primary means of favorably influencing public opinion is often by becoming a "partner in infamy." Reagan uses the same tactics in discrediting the media as he does in discrediting his opponents. "As Floyd Abrams, the famed constitutional lawyer, observes, the Administration is 'attacking the legitimacy of the press, not its performance.' "[22] This kind of rhetoric, while not unique to Ronald Reagan, is present throughout the Reagan years, but as Table 1.2 indicates, it is most prevalent during elections and crises. Examples of this tactic include statements like, "Contrary to what was portrayed and widely heralded in these last few weeks . . ."[23] and ". . . some of you in the media misinterpreted and have declared that I claimed that you could call back a bomb or a submarine missile and never did I ever. . . ."[24]

Given the fact that Reagan is a popular president and that the media have been under increasing criticism in recent years, rhetoric like this does much to reinforce the public's perception of how the media do their job, and even the nature of that job. Everyone, at one time or another, has felt misrepresented. With a president in office who is skilled at conveying righteous indignation at the media's approach to his presidency, and with a media afraid of "backlash," it is no wonder that the media were increasingly "soft" on the president.[25]

Evasion

It is even more difficult for the media to be "tough" because the public often confuses presidential visibility with media access to the president. As Sam Donaldson points out, members of the media often yell questions at Reagan because they are not allowed close enough to ask them in a civil manner. Yet the public continually receives images of the president seemingly surrounded by the media corps and conclude that he is, in fact, accessible. The media are therefore by implication guilty of misrepresentation when they claim otherwise, and the White House wins another battle in the "credibility war."[26] Again, this kind of positioning is not unique to Reagan, but its use has become increasingly sophisticated and its consequences increasingly clear during the Reagan administration.

This difficulty in forcing accountability on an unwilling president is compounded by his use of humor, stories, and anecdotes. He uses this tactic less in interview situations than in his speeches,[27] but it appears consistently, most notably when he is deflecting a series of questions designed to pin him down to a specific statement.[28] This reinforces the perception of a kindly and gentle man beleaguered by an aggressive and unruly media. "The press found itself completely unable to deal with Reagan in the usual way. His mock humility, his seemingly total amiability, and his appearance as the big, rich, smiling daddy for whom the voters had yearned so long ..."[29] made the established routine of press/presidential relations impossible.

This is the key to much of Reagan's rhetorical control of the media. He puts them in a position whereby if they respond on his terms, they are hampered in doing their jobs. If they respond on other terms, they play into his portrayal of them as the "bad guys." Either way, they are kept off balance, on the defensive, and unable to respond in their routinized ways. By reducing the ability of reporters and their organizations to respond to his presidency in their normal patterned ways, Reagan made it increasingly possible to establish new patterns of behavior and response. These new patterns were designed to expedite the administration's control of the media and the news, and to decrease the media's ability to perform their "watchdog" function.[30]

Another important tactic in Reagan's rhetorical control of the media is deflection. Reagan's answers to questions put by the press include, "I can't answer that, it's still under review"; "We're still waiting for details"; or simply, "I don't know." This has several effects. First, if the media keep pressing for details, they appear to be hounding the president. None of us like to say, "I don't know"; admissions of ignorance come hard to everyone. To be in the position of admitting to ignorance again and again inevitably creates a situation in which the public will be sympathetic to the president, and not to the media. As Carroll Kirkpatrick, retired columnist of the *Washington Post* says, " ... the public doesn't sympathize with the reporter who asks some nasty question; they sympathize with the president more often than not."[31] This puts the media in the position of having to choose between getting an answer to a question that the president should know the answer to at the cost of being perceived as monsters or of accepting the president's admission of ignorance, which may or may not be legitimate. And stories that had as their theme the president's ignorance were not received favorably, or with much attention.[32]

The second consequence of this tactic is that the president is in the position of looking as if he is active on a variety of fronts; it occasionally appeared as if he and his staff were doing nothing but studying various policies, positions, and programs. But the results of these studies were very rarely forthcoming. Reagan could put off the media and delay the day of reckoning, which, with luck and control of the agenda, might never come.

This tactic was particularly effective in foreign policy and, most particularly, when combined with the technique of the symbolic response. This is a tactic that Reagan has long employed to his advantage.[33] Unlike in his prepresidential rhetoric, in the presidential documents studied here Reagan primarily uses symbolic responses in regard to foreign rather than domestic policy issues. (In his prepresidential period, he used them equally in regard to both arenas.) Discussions of foreign policy lend themselves to the kinds of grand moral positioning that Reagan excels at. In response to a question on the SALT II Treaty in 1981, Reagan replied, " . . . if the SALT II Treaty had been ratified, it would have permitted the Soviet Union to add to its arsenal nuclear explosive power equal to what we dropped on Hiroshima every 11 minutes for the life of the SALT II Treaty."[34] And on SDI in 1984:

> My ambition, or my dream, for—if there is a defensive weapon— you see, here's a weapon in the world and for the first time it is a weapon that has no defense against it, except deterrence, that we each have it. It's like two fellows with a gun pointed at each other, both with their fingers on the trigger, and we're going to stand, spend the rest of our life doing that.[35]

Reagan is also skilled at the use of direct evasions to direct questions. These evasions often come in the form of answering a question that he was not asked and ignoring the one he was asked. In 1981, for instance, when asked about the details of the AWACS agreement, Reagan shifted the focus of the question and began discussing the use of AWACS during the Lebanon crisis.[36] In 1986, he took a similar approach to a question on the effect of oil prices on exploration, answering as if the question addressed the importance of U.S. business productivity.[37]

This tactic is a particulary frustrating one for the media, leading as it does to presidential domination of the agenda. For when the president answers questions that he was not asked and ignores the ones he was asked, the media are in the position of having to frame questions in so precise a manner that the only possible answer is one that addresses the question. This is extraordinarily difficult to do; to do it in the context of a press conference is bad enough, to do it when you are squeezing questions in at photo opportunities or over the sound of a helicopter rotor is very nearly impossible.

Another form of evasion is to simply deny the questioner's right to ask the question. " 'You can't let your people know' what the government is doing, the President explained at a news conference, 'without letting the wrong people know—those who are in opposition to what you're doing.' "[38] This, of course, brings up the question of who, then, is allowed to question the White House? The answer of the Reagan administration seems to be, "only those who are not likely to."

Still another form of deflection is the historical or personal evasion. A reporter asking a question on the new budget proposals in 1981 was liable to get a response dealing with Reagan's record as governor of California[39] or a story about his personal life.[40] The reporter, faced with an answer that has no relevance to his question, can only repeat the question and be faced with the response, "I've answered that already." Contradicting the president is not as difficult for the national media as it is for most of us, but it still does not occur very often, particularly as it becomes clear that it decreases goodwill without producing any results.

His final deflecting tactic is to refer to or cite others to take the heat off of himself.[41] Reagan can stand there smiling while others are forced to respond to difficult questions. By 1983, that technique tended to hurt Reagan more than it helped in terms of his media coverage—it became "news" that the president didn't know what was going on in his own administration, and use of the tactic declined. Here, the change in the political environment is key. Reagan's rhetorical tactics, like anyone's, are effective only under certain circumstances and given certain conditions. When these conditions change, the utility and effectiveness of his tactics also change.

Staging

As far as staging is concerned, the device most commonly cited is the restriction of the presidential press conference.

Where Lyndon Lyndon B. Johnson averaged as many as 26.1 a year, and even Richard Nixon held 6.5 a year, Ronald Reagan, neither at war abroad nor beleaguered at home, managed only 6.5 a year, less than any modern president.[42] In addition, when Reagan did hold press conferences, they were changed from afternoons to prime time to maximize his exposure to the public and minimize the role of the media.[43] The press is also rigidly and ceremonially controlled during a Reagan press conference. As one author reports:

> To take one example, the presidential press conference has become a unique, ritualistic form of communication that blends elements from political and denominational sources. President Reagan chooses to enter the room from an open doorway, striding down a red carpet that leads to the podium. The doorway and red carpet provide a dramatic background as he speaks and at the close of the press conference he turns and exits down the long red carpet through a doorway at the end of the room. The visual image as seen by the television viewer resembles that of a Protestant minister. . . . The President delivers his "homily," opens up the conference for questions . . . and the ceremony ends.[44]

While aimed at a television audience, this staging must also have an effect on the reporters, both as witnesses themselves and as they are aware of what the audience is seeing. Few of us are comfortable questioning a minister—particularly when he is still in his pulpit, and most particularly when the questioner must remain seated and raise his hand for recognition by the higher authority. This atmosphere clearly does much to reduce the combativeness of the media and increase presidential control.[45]

Secrecy

In addition to presidential control of the media at preess conferences, the Reagan adminstration has displayed a "passion for secrecy" in its dealings with both the press and the public.[46] In November 1983, the *New York Times* charged administration officials with disseminating "much inaccurate information and many unproved assertions. They did so while withholding significant facts and impeding efforts by the journalists to verify official statements."[47] Helen Thomas, senior White House wire service correspondent, believes that

> Many of the reforms that grew out of the nightmare that was Watergate have been eliminated or will be if Reagan has his way. The drive has been systematic to cut down legitimate access to news in the foreign policy field. New regulations have been devised to tighten the circle of those with access to top secret documents. The Freedom of Information Act is under siege, and Reagan's forces seek to legitimate domestic spying by the CIA.[48]

Observers agree that systematic efforts to control the media are not original with Ronald Reagan; they also agree that because of the growth in the White House Press Office[49] and an improved understanding of how to make and define news,[50] conditions under Reagan have gotten significantly worse. It is hardly possible, for instance, that under any of our previous presidents a press secretary could show such contempt for the media as to place on his desk a sign that reads, "You don't tell us how to stage the news, and we don't tell you how to cover it." Larry Speakes did.[51]

In sum, this chapter has revealed certain rhetorical tools and tactics used by Ronald Reagan in his dealings with the media that decreased their control over the dissemination of the news and increased the ability of the White House to command the kind of coverage he desired.

CONCLUSIONS

The president helps set the U.S. agenda. In so doing, he helps to structure the ways in which Americans think about issues, events, and other political actors. While no single person controls the American public's perceptions, when the president speaks in a strong and consistent voice over time, there can be no doubt that he has a very influential voice. This is particularly true when historical circumstances favor the message the president is sending.

This was true during the Reagan administration. Given a climate personally favorable to him and antagonistic to the media, Reagan was quick to seize the advantage and act to curtail the access and legitimacy of the White House media corps. This does not mean that the media are innocent bystanders or the protectors of democracy and should be rescued from the infamous Reagan administration. The question of the proper role of the media in our national politics is a complex subject and deserves more attention than I have given it here. What this study has shown is that through his public rhetoric as well as through organizational and legal means, Reagan has positioned himself in such a way as to discredit his opposition and the media.

Rhetoric does not control events; it serves to interpret them. Through a combination of organizational techniques and rhetorical positioning, Reagan helped to structure situations so that his interpretation, already in a favorable position, would be paramount. The nature of that interpretation, as well as further extrapolation of Reagan's rhetorical tactics and techniques, provide the substance of the following three chapters.

NOTES

Part of this Chapter was originally presented at the Annual Meeting of the Midwest Political Science Association, Chicago, Ill., April 1988.

1. As quoted by Martin Linsky, *Impact: How the Press Affects Federal Policymaking* (New York: W. W. Norton, 1986), p. 17.

2. Linsky, *Impact*, p. 3.

3. David Morgan, *The Capital Press Corps: Newsmen and the Governing of New York State* (Westport, Conn.: Greenwood Press, 1978), p. 148.

4. William L. Rivers, *The Other Government: Power and the Washington Media* (New York: Universe Books, 1982), p. 10.

5. George F. Will, "Introduction," in *Press, Politics, and Popular Government*, ed. George F. Will (Washington, D.C.: The American Enterprise Institute, 1972), p. 2.

6. Robert L. Bartley, "The Press: Adversary, Surrogate Sovereign, or Both?," in *Press, Politics, and Popular Government*, ed. George F. Will (Washington, D.C.: The American Enterprise Institute, 1972), p. 7.

7. John Tebbel and Sarah Miles Watts, *The Press and the Presidency: From George Washington to Ronald Reagan* (New York, Oxford: Oxford University Press, 1985), p. 549.

8. James Reston, "How to Fool the People: Reagan's No-Fault Politics," New York *Times*, October 5, 1986, p. E21.

9. Dom Bonafede, "Scandal Time," *National Journal* 19 (January 24, 1987): 199–200, 205–7.

10. Walter Karp, "Liberty under Siege: The Reagan Administration's Taste for Autocracy," *Harper's* (November 1985): 53–67; See also Tebbel and Watts, *Press and the Presidency*, p. 543.

11. See, for example, Alexis de Tocqueville, *Democracy in America*, ed. J. P. Meyer (New York: Anchor Books, 1969); Benjamin I. Page, *Choices and Echoes in Presidential Elections* (Chicago: University of Chicago Press, 1978), pp. 31–32; and Donald J. Devine, *The Political Culture of the United States* (Boston: Little, Brown and Co., 1972).

12. Alexander Cockburn and James Ridgeway, "The World of Appearance: The Public Campaign," in *The Hidden Election: Politics and Economics in the 1980 Presidential Campaign*, eds. Thomas Ferguson and Joel Rogers (New York: Pantheon Books, 1981), p. 65.

13. Sam Donaldson, *Hold On, Mr. President!* (New York: Fawcett Crest, 1987), p. 10.

14. "Remarks to Reporters" without question and answer sessions were deleted; they are more representative of Reagan's public speech than of his dealings and relationship with the press.

15. The same argument applies to these speeches as to "Remarks"; those with no question and answer session were deleted.

16. Larry Speakes with Robert Pack, *Speaking Out: Inside the Reagan White House* (New York: Charles Scribner's Sons, 1988), p. 65.

17. For examples, see "Exchange with Reporters," *Public Papers of the President* (hereafter cited as *Public Papers*), May 7, 1982, Washington, D.C.: U.S. Government Printing Office); "Excerpt from an Interview with Ann Devroy of the Gannett News Service," *Public Papers*, August 24, 1983; "The President's News Conference," *Public Papers*, May 22, 1984.

18. See "Remarks and a Question and Answer Session with Reporters," *Public Papers*, March 21, 1983; "Interview" with *USA Today, Public Papers*, April 26, 1983; "Interview with Reporters," *Public Papers*, December 23, 1983.

19. See, for examples, "Interview" with Jeremiah O'Leary of the *Washington Times, Public Papers*, August 13, 1982; "Interview" with Ann Devroy of *USA Today, Public Papers*, March 29, 1984; "The President's Today News Conference," *Public Papers*, March 21, 1985.

20. See, for example, "Address Before a Joint Session of the Congress on the Program for Economic Recovery," *Public Papers*, February 18, 1981; "Remarks at the Mid-Winter Congressional City Conference of

the National League of Cities," *Public Papers*, March 2, 1981; "Remarks and a Question and Answer Session with Reporters at the Fiscal Year 1983 Budget Signing Ceremony," *Public Papers*, February 8, 1982.

21. See Chapter 2 for a more detailed discussion of this point.

22. Karp, "Liberty," p. 66; see also Tebbel and Watts, *Press and the Presidency*, p. 544.

23. "The President's News Conference," *Public Papers*, February 18, 1982.

24. "Interview" with Bruce Drake of the New York *Daily News*, *Public Papers*, July 8, 1986. for other examples, see "Interview" with members of the Editorial Board of the New York *Post*, *Public Papers*, March 23, 1982; "Exchange with Reporters," April 15, 1982; "The President's News Conference," *Public Papers*, June 11, 1986.

25. Rivers, *Other Government*, p. 21.

26. Donaldson, *Hold On*, p. 145.

27. Mary E. Stuckey, *Getting Into the Game: The Pre-Presidential Rhetoric of Ronald Reagan* (New York: Praeger, 1989).

28. See, for example, "Informal Exchange With Reporters," *Public Papers*, March 18, 1985; "Question and Answer Session With Reporters," *Public Papers*, April 5, 1982; "Interview" with reporters from the Los Angeles *Times, Public Papers*, January 20, 1982; "The President's News Conference," *Public Papers*, March 21, 1985.

29. Tebbel and Watts, *Press and the Presidency*, p. 536.

30. Speakes, *Speaking Out*, p. 217.

31. Kenneth W. Thompson, ed., *Ten Presidents and the Press* (Washington, D.C.: University Press of America, 1980), p. 92.

32. Floyd Abrams, "The New Effort to Control Information," New York *Times Magazine*, September 25, 1983, pp. 22–23.

33. Stuckey, *Getting into the Game*, p. 54.

34. "Interview" with the Los Angeles *Times*, January 20, 1982.

35. "Interview" with the *Wall Street Journal*, *Public Papers*, February 2, 1984. For other examples, see "The President's News Conference," *Public Papers*, January 5, 1983; "Exchange With Reporters on Terrorism," *Public Papers*, January 18, 1982; and "Interview with Representatives of the Baltimore Sun," *Public Papers*, March 12, 1986.

36. "Exchange With Reporters," *Public Papers*, September 25, 1981.

37. "Remarks and a Question and Answer Session with the American Society of Newspaper Editors," *Public Papers*, April 9, 1986.

38. Karp, "Liberty," p. 61.

39. For examples, see "Remarks and a Question and Answer Session on the Program for Economic Recovery at a Breakfast for Newspaper and Television News Editors," *Public Papers*, February 19, 1981; "Re-

marks with a Question and Answer Session With Reporters," *Public Papers*, January 14, 1983.

40. See "The President's News Conference," *Public Papers*, February 16, 1983; "1984 Presidential Debate," *Public Papers*, October 7, 1984; "Remarks and a Question and Answer Session with Regional Editors and Broadcasters," *Public Papers*, April 18, 1985.

41. This is a tactic favored by Eisenhower as well. See Fred I. Greenstein, *The Hidden-Hand Presidency: Eisenhower as Leader* (New York: Basic Books, 1982).

42. John M. Orman, "Reagan's Imperial Presidency," (Paper delivered at the Annual Meeting of the American Political Science Association, Chicago, Ill., August 1987).

43. Tebbel and Watts, *Press and the Presidency*, p. 545. It is important to note that this is neither original to nor confined to the Reagan administration. Many presidents have found advantages in going directly to the people, and evening press conferences are not of recent vintage. The key difference here is one of degree rather than of kind.

44. Gregor Goethals, "Religious Communication and Popular Piety," *Journal of Communications*, Vol. 35, No. 1 (1985): 149–56.

45. Tebbel and Watts, *Press and the Presidency*, p. 537.

46. Orman, "Reagan's Imperial Presidency," p. 5.

47. Cited by Tebbel and Watts, *Press and the Presidency*, p. 543.

48. Helen Thomas, "Ronald Reagan and the Management of News," in *The White House Press on the Presidency*, ed. Kenneth W. Thompson (Latham: University Press of America, 1983), pp. 37–38.

49. Tebbel and Watts, *Press and the Presidency*, p. 537.

50. Tebbel and Watts, *Press and the Presidency*, p. 537. See also Morgan, *Capital Press*, p. 151; Rivers, *Other Government*, p. 58n1; Abrams, "New Effort," pp. 22–23; Laurien Alexandre, "In the Service of the State: Public Diplomacy, Government, Media, and Ronald Reagan," *Media, Culture, and Society*, Vol. 1, No. 9 (1987): 29–46; and Thompson, *Ten Presidents*, p. 88.

51. Tebbel and Watts, *Press and the Presidency*, p. 552.

Chapter 2

Revolution: Reagan's First Years, 1981–1982

INTRODUCTION

This chapter covers Ronald Reagan's rhetoric during his formative years as president, when he was learning the job and applying various strategies associated with it. Consequently, while Reagan's early years were characterized by some spectacular and well-known successes, the Reagan White House was also guilty of some fairly serious blunders. The success of Reagan's rhetoric was thus highly variable as he learned which strategies worked and which did not.

Another important aspect of the Reagan rhetoric during this period is the substance rather than the presentation. The most notable aspect of Reagan's rhetoric between 1981–1982 is the lack of foreign policy statements and speeches. He did not give a foreign policy speech until October 15, 1981, and the quantity of foreign policy rhetoric remained low throughout the period. The reasons for this and the consequences that resulted from it can best be understood when Reagan's speech is placed within the political context he faced.

The data for this period include all of Ronald Reagan's public speeches in excess of one page in length. There were 157 total documents for 1981 and 278 for 1982, with a total of 435 documents for the period. The number of documents is larger for

1982, reflecting Reagan's participation in mid-term congressional campaigns.

POLITICAL CONTEXT, 1981–1982

When one looks back at the early years of Reagan's first term, one remembers the budget success, the AWACs deal, and Reagan's personal courage following the attempt on his life. The other side of those early years—the "presidency of the rich" and "Queen Nancy," Reagan's foreign policy confusion and "evil empire" rhetoric, and the 1983 recession—provide dimmer memories. But to understand Reagan's administration and the political rhetoric that formed an important part of that administraton, those events must be placed within a political context. The "teflon presidency" was not created in a vacuum, nor was it invented out of whole cloth. The rhetoric and image management that composed the seeming invincibility of Reagan's popularity were designed in response to specific events and with specific goals in mind. In order to understand those goals, we must take a brief look at the events.

Despite the fact that Reagan won a decisive victory over Jimmy Carter in 1980, the nature and extent of his mandate to govern was unclear. Many analysts, in fact, consider the vote a clear rejection of Carter and a vote for change rather than a positive endorsement of Ronald Reagan.[1] Reagan, however, was quick to claim a mandate and to act upon it. With the support of the media, Reagan was off to an impressive beginning.[2]

Five factors contribute to his success: Reagan's staffing; his limited legislative priorities; party discipline in Congress; the support of the media; and the president's response to the assassination attempt. First and most important is Reagan's staff, particularly the "Troika," composed of "Baker the organizer, and Deaver the protector of the Reagans. Ed Meese was the policy man."[3] Meese and Deaver had worked with Reagan for years and understood his priorities. They also had his confidence and were able to look after him politically as well as personally. Members of the Troika were particularly known for their understanding of the media and their ability to use those media to the president's advantage. As Lawrence Barrett points out, the Troika was well versed in the connection between public "perception and political power."[4]

Equally important, Reagan's advisors maintained strong control over the paper flow within the White House.[5] This allowed Reagan to set the ideological agenda without having to worry about the substantive, policy side of things, and helped to keep intraadministration conflict to a minimum. Decision making appeared orderly and controlled due to the Troika's ability to put an effective lid on internal administrative battles and conflicts.

The second factor contributing to Reagan's early success is the limited number of priorities in the first year. When asked about his priorities soon after the election, Reagan replied, "The economy, the economy, and the economy." Reagan put all of his eggs in the budget basket, which while risky, also promised a big payoff if he could come through. Due to a strong lobbying effort in Congress and broad-based public support for "giving the president's program a chance,"[6] come through he did. The 1981 budget success helped create the impression of a president who meant business and who had the political ability to do business.

The third factor contributing to Reagan's early success is his ability to control Congress. A Republican majority in the Senate was certainly a help, as was any representative's understandable reluctance to oppose a popular president. The Republicans also did well in the House elections, losing only three seats. Because of this, even northern Republicans, who could usually be counted on by the Democrats, were lost, as were the southern Democrats.[7] The result was a substantial de facto majority willing to support the president. That this majority would begin to erode as early as 1982 in no way dampened its early effectiveness. That early effectiveness provided another boost to Reagan's image as an irresistible force.

This image, as transmitted—some would argue created—by the mass media, is the fourth factor in Reagan's early success. Despite the fact that Reagan's public standing was low, his standing in the Washington community "was obviously very different."[8] Michael Baruch Grossman and Martha Joynt Kumar attribute this difference to the administration's "ability to deal with media insiders."[9] These insiders helped foster the impression around Washington that Reagan was a force to be contended with. Widespread belief in this image helped make Reagan such a force:

> Reagan's first six months in office were consistently covered by the president watchers as the days of the "Super President." The early successes of the Reagan administration were portrayed by the media as "victories" over Congress. These included victories with respect to tax cuts, domestic spending cuts, increased defense spending, and AWACs to Saudi Arabia. Most important for the establishment of the "Super President" myth, Reagan survived an assassination attempt in his first year.[10]

Given low expectations of Washington insiders, the media, and the country as a whole,[11] Reagan benefitted not only from the sympathy he gained as a result of being shot, but also from evidence that he was in touch with his administration.[12] As Lou Cannon says:

> The attempt on Reagan's life had, in fact, many results. In the short run, it produced a wave of popular sympathy which assisted the passage of Reagan's economic legislation. In the middle distance, it slowed Reagan's learning curve on foreign policy and encouraged his inclination to over-delegate. And in the long run, Reagan's grace under pressure destroyed forever any lingering doubts that the President was a cardboard man whose aspirations and inspirations were as synthetic as a celluloid screen. The heroism reflected in Reagan's humor was genuine, and everyone knew it.[33]

After the attempt on his life, Reagan's popularity shot up ten points, and on his return, he was greeted by Congress in what one analyst calls a "lovefest."[14] The attempted assassination made it even more difficult for Congress to oppose the president, and the less they opposed him, the more invincible he appeared.

But even while these five factors, working together, contributed to Reagan's early success, that success was not unqualified, and he had both substantive and image problems in these first years. The substantive problems of the first two years centered on the economy. "Reaganomics," instead of saving the country from a "financial mess," resulted in a recession. The recession, combined with David Stockman's revelations of November 1981 published in the *Atlantic Monthly* about the budget projections and the "magic asterisk" undermined much of Reagan's 1981 support.[15] The substantive problem of the recession would not have been so bad, but for the image problem of the Reagan White House: "The Reagan White House became a symbol of the New Extravagance at the moment it was asking Americans to make due with fewer government benefits . . . making the contrast between high times in Washington and hard times in the country all the more stark."[16]

The contrast between the way in which the Reagans lived—with Nancy's designer gowns, new china, and fondness for millionaires—and the hardships faced by growing numbers of citizens resulted in a serious image problem for the Reagan White House. The early "spin patrol" got busy; Nancy was photographed with foster grandparents and became an opponent of drug abuse. But the effect was limited. Reagan may have proved that the American people want their president to "own a suit," but they don't want him to appear too comfortable in a tuxedo either. In this regard, the Reagan's trips to the ranch were invaluable in adding a "common touch" to what was otherwise in danger of being a "rich man's presidency."

The story of the early days of Reagan's term is a positive one, full of success with Congress. It is also the story of a foreign policy that was "more of a stance than a policy,"[17] an unfulfilled "New Right" social agenda, and potential image problems for both himself and the First Lady. Surprising ground for a teflon presidency to be built upon. It is somewhat less surprising, however, when we look at the rhetoric of these years, and note how Reagan positioned himself in the face of these successes and potential problems. For his rhetorical handling of these early events made the teflon presidency possible.

RONALD REAGAN'S RHETORIC, 1981–1982

There are many themes running through Reagan's early presidential rhetoric. Many of these themes are consistent with or identical to his prepresidential style. Two of these themes, however, take on an added significance in the context of presidential speech and are the foundation for the strengths and weaknesses of Reagan's presidential rhetoric. The first of these is his use of inclusive and exclusive rhetoric. The second is Reagan's rhetorical reliance upon heroes.

Just as in his prepresidential speech, Reagan relies heavily upon the tactics of inclusion and exclusion during his early years as president. He uses these rhetorical tactics to separate the audience from his opponents and to attach them to himself and his policies. Both tactics involve a variety of strategies used in complex ways.

Inclusion and Exclusion

When using the tactic of inclusion, Reagan's main approach is to view the audience as a symbol, based either upon their agreement with him or upon their values. When using the audience as symbol, Reagan picks one characteristic of the audience and uses it to show how that audience is emblematic of the nation as a whole. This characteristic is either their belief in Ronald Reagan or some uniquely "American" value that they alone fully exemplify.

When viewing the audience as special because of their agreement with Reagan, his rhetoric emphasizes both their importance as a group and their closeness to the president. This particular approach, which Reagan used 22 times between his inauguration and the end of 1982, is most common during election stump speeches. It is an important tactic, because the audience is allowed to feel as if they are a special and unique part of the America that Reagan is so proud of; without them, Reagan would not be able to do the things that will help bring "America back." The audience thus has a vested interest in believing and supporting Reagan, for without him, they do not get to feel special. With him, they are reminded that they "are making history," that the president needs "your help, your unity more than ever," and that "everything we Americans hold dear is safer because of what you are doing."[18] All of these appeals help to solidify support for a variety of the president's positions without his ever having to explicitly discuss those positions. This does not imply that his audiences are stupid, nor does it imply that they cannot see political speech making for what it is. What it does indicate is that people are predisposed to support the president; he makes that support easier through this kind of rhetoric, which can solidify support and perhaps disarm some criticism.

The second tactic associated with inclusion is Reagan's reliance upon values. In this case, it is not the audience's agreement with or support of the president that makes them important and special, it is the values that they symbolize. This is a favorite theme when Reagan speaks before Hispanic audiences: "But seriously, all of this has given me a deep appreciation of Hispanic culture, including its music, food, and qualities, but more than that, it engenders especially, the sense of personal honor and integrity. . . . Today, all of us are rediscovering those values, but the Hispanic community never lost them."[19]

This rhetoric says two things to the audience: that the things important to them are also important to the speaker, and that Ronald Reagan appreciates values that are important to the audience. That audience is worthy of Reagan's time, not just for their votes, but because of their intrinsic value. This can be particularly important for minority communities, who are not being appreciated despite their culture and values, but because of them.

The flip side to this positive and inclusive rhetoric is the rhetoric of exclusion. When using this tactic, Reagan is attempting to separate the audience from people or ideas that he disagrees with. He does this in a variety of ways: He undermines the competence of the opposition; he undermines the motives of the opposition; or he simply defines the opposition as "other," "un-American" and therefore "bad." He says, for example, that "There is a great reluctance on the part of the Federal Government to trust the people out there, and they believe that inhaling the fogs off the Potomac imparts a wisdom that is not generally shared."[20]

Just as he did in his prepresidential rhetoric, Reagan as president is fond of characterizing his opposition in less-than-flattering terms. They are "children" or backward in some way.

There is much that they don't understand. "Those who still advocate far-removed Federal solutions are dinosaurs, mindlessly carrying on as they always have, unaware that times have changed."[21] This has the double effect of demeaning the opposition while exalting Reagan. For if they don't understand, who does? Why Reagan does, naturally. He can bring truth and guidance.

His guidance can be trusted, because he relies upon the principles that our nation was founded upon. "Sometimes it seems that we've strayed from that noble beginning, from our conviction that standards of right and wrong do exist and must be lived up to."[22] In basing his rhetoric on our first principles, Reagan has chosen a nearly unimpeachable source of legitimacy. Not many Americans, and no American politician, will argue with the Founders. And few people will listen to a debate upon the meaning of the Founders' words. So long as the context is patriotic, the interpretation is likely to go unquestioned.

This is even more powerful when Reagan unites the return to first principles with clear-cut choices. There is no ambiguity and very little complexity in Reagan's rhetoric. Much of its appeal, in fact, lies in his insistence that the world is not really all that complex and that technology has not mattered all that much. This insistence upon "simple answers" makes his arguments easy to follow, emotionally evocative, and difficult to refute.

For example, Reagan often argues from definition,[23] and his definitions depend upon the comparison of two opposing and uncomplicated elements. This is clearest in his discussion of the Soviet Union, but it has been a favorite tactic in domestic affairs as well. He defines his economic program, for example, as "completely different form the artificial quick fixes of the past."[24]

In undermining the motives of the opposition, Reagan is more direct. He makes it quite clear that the people who oppose him are not really well intentioned but stupid; they are actually petty, spiteful, politically motivated, and unworthy of any consideration. He says, for example:

> After you got back from your break and I got back from mine, some people developed a bad case of the jitters. Of all things, they were blaming the high interest rates and the other economic

ills on the program you'd just passed a few weeks before. Of course, they'd had a little help in arriving at that idea; most of those making the fuss never supported the program in the first place. And they also know darn well that it doesn't even go into effect until the day after tomorrow. I suppose by sundown the day after tomorrow they'll be saying, "See, we told you so."[25]

In addition, Reagan continually criticized "those Monday morning quarterbacks who insist our program hasn't worked,"[26] and filled his speeches with comments like, "I don't know about you, but I'm getting tired of whining voices telling us we can't do this, we can't do that. . . ."[27] Another example of Reagan's criticism is his exhortation not to "be fooled by wild charges,"[28] made by people who scare older Americans,[29] lie to black Americans,[30] and attempt to delude female Americans.[31]

There are others, however, even more dangerous than Reagan's outspoken critics. Those others pose "the real threat to the recovery" because they are both small-minded and selfishly motivated. They

oppose only a small part of the overall program, while supporting the overall effort. Needless to say, the small portion that these parochial groups oppose always deals with the cuts that affect them directly. Those cuts they oppose. They favor cutting everyone else's subsidy as an important step in cutting inflation and getting the country moving again.[32]

It is interesting to note here that Reagan uses "liberal" rhetoric to promote conservative causes and succeeds in undermining the entire liberal agenda in the process. He is the spokesman for change, for opportunity, for a willingness to experiment, for optimism, and the "end of gloom and doom."

This gives Reagan's opponents two choices: They can oppose everything in the program and be considered "dinosaurs"; or they oppose only pieces of it and be parochial, selfish, and hypocritical. Neither of these positions is tenable. Because of their motivations, these critics cannot be trusted. The consequences of listening to these false prophets are immediate and clearly negative. "Attempts to saddle this administration with the blame for economic problems long-in-the-making only sink our economy deeper into the quagmire of partisan debate."[33] Reagan pictures himself as a nonpolitical creature, single-mindedly involved in the national interest. Politics is dirty and unpleasant, but he occasionally involves himself out of necessity.

This does not mean that all of the criticism aimed at Reagan and his programs was rational, accurate, and made without political motivation. Not at all. But to characterize all of his opposition in such demeaning terms, and to impute the competence or motives of anyone who disagreed with the White House, is perhaps understandable, but cannot be considered ideal democratic rhetoric. In democracies, more than in any other kind of system, it is imperative that we keep the lines of communication open. This kind of rhetoric, which discourages respect for your opponents, does not foster the kind of debate essential to democracies. This point will resurface in Chapter 5. What needs to be noted here is that Reagan is attempting to structure debate along the lines of "us" and "them"; if you are not one of "us," you are automatically and unquestionably one of "them." It is precisely this aspect of his rhetoric that will cause him difficulty later.

Reagan's Heroes

In all of his presidential speeches, Reagan relies heavily upon the theme of the American hero. This theme arises 28 times during this period. It is an effective tactic, for it allows Reagan to speak with the upbeat optimism that he favors and that makes him so easy to listen to. It comes in two parts: great deeds and great men.

In the great deeds scenario, Reagan allows the audience to be full participants in the important problems that are being faced and the important tasks that must be completed. In his first inaugural, for example, he talks of "sacrifice" and "requirements." What is required of the audience, however, is no real sacrifice, no action at all. All that is required is a belief "in ourselves . . . our capacity to perform great deeds."[34] But members of the audience are not called upon to participate in any of these great deeds, merely to believe in their capacity to perform them.

This distinguishes Reagan's speech from that of a John Kennedy, for example. For when Kennedy demanded that we "ask not what our country can do for you, but what you can do for your country," he was beckoning people to service. The Peace Corps and VISTA were examples of the "asking" Kennedy required. Reagan's call to duty is hollow, for he does not really expect anyone to serve; he does not really ask for sacrifice. Kennedy sounded a challenge. Reagan both challenges and answers the challenge in the same speech, almost in the same moment. A challenge that is so easily answered is essentially unsatisfying. And the inspiration that is offered through such a challenge is also essentially hollow and unsatisfying.

This may well be, in fact, what lies at the root of Reagan's inability to effect any moral change in America, to bring us back to the first principles that are so important in his rhetoric. He isn't really trying to effect that change; it is simply good theater.

By exalting heroes whose conduct symbolizes the best in all of us, this dynamic is reinforced. We all get to be heroes; we are all like the people in Reagan's speeches. The price that we pay for this vicarious heroism is, however, a cheapening of the heroic concept. For instead of offering examples of extraordinary bravery or achievement, examples that could serve to inspire us, to make us strive in some way, Reagan offers us examples of what we are already like by virtue of being American.[35] This, like the examples of great deeds, proves to be hollow inspiration.

But it is not without its price, both for the American polity and for Ronald Reagan. The price for the polity is that when all that is required is belief without challenge, politics becomes just another spectator sport—and an uninteresting one to boot. This kind of "feel-good Americanism" may be soothing for a while, but will eventually become uninteresting. If audiences want to feel good about America in this way, shows like "MacGyver" and "Mission Impossible" are a better deal than a presidential news conference or speech.

The consequences for Reagan were much more severe. For it is this kind of rhetoric that provided the base for the teflon presidency, and when that base proved unstable, it very nearly brought the president down.

TEFLON RHETORIC

One of the clearest facts about Reagan's early rhetoric is the almost total absence of foreign policy. He did not give a major foreign policy speech until October 15, 1981, fully ten months after his inauguration.[36] In the intervening months, Reagan's foreign policy staff was disorganized, confused, and almost continually at odds internally.[37] Reagan's only public comments on foreign policy were brief, given in reaction to current events rather than of an agenda-setting nature, and did not give the impression of a president who was either knowledgeable or in control.[38] By June, Reagan was so beleaguered on foreign policy that the press were asking him whether or not he had one. His response is illustrative: "Well, there seems to be a feeling as if an address on foreign policy is somehow evidence that you have a foreign policy, and until you make an address, you don't have one. And I challenge that. I'm satisfied that we do have a foreign policy."[39] This from the most public president the United States has ever seen is quite a statement.

It is only later in Reagan's early years that he begins to focus on foreign policy, a fact that can be accounted for in several ways. First, foreign policy requires a learning period. Given both his newness to national government and the effects of the assassination attempt, Reagan's learning was delayed. Second, Reagan's first priority was the economic measures, many of which were passed in 1981. His success with Congress in getting the budget and tax cuts passed, along with increases in defense spending, was largely a product of his single-minded devotion to his economic program.[40] Finally, it is altogether possible that Reagan said nothing about foreign policy because he had nothing to say. The foreign policy world is for Reagan quite clear and quite simple. It is East against West, and the West will win—provided we are adequately armed—because we are morally superior. For Reagan this amounted to a foreign policy.

This became a useful foreign policy in 1982, when the recession and worries about further effects of Reaganomics combined to hurt Reagan in the popularity polls. While the president's interpretation of events is probably the loudest and most important in the field of domestic affairs, it is not the only interpretation. And Reagan's budget cuts ensured that other interpretations would abound. Not only were other interpretations available, but the sources of those interpretations were, despite Reagan's best efforts, often credible. They came from other politicians, the church, and the leaders of civil rights and other groups, and they were united in their opposition to Reaganism.

One fact about foreign policy stands out. In terms of foreign affairs, the president's is the clearest, strongest, and often the only voice. Presidents not only control, to a large degree, the foreign policy agenda, but also the public interpretation of that agenda. So it is not surprising that from the early days of 1982, Reagan turned increasing amounts of his attention to foreign policy.

Specifically, out of a total of 87 foreign policy documents made during these years, 29 of them are from 1981 and 58—exactly double that number—are from 1982.[41] In addition to an increase in number, the content of Reagan's foreign policy statements also began to change.

In the first place, by mid-1982 his statements began to the less reactive and more agenda-setting. His Caribbean Basin Initiative and trip to Europe largely account for this change, but the number of purely ceremonial foreign policy exchanges also decreases (from 17 in 1981 to 9 in 1982). In part, this is due to the necessity of a new president greeting heads of state, a necessity that was over by 1982. In part, however, it is also due to the new president becoming comfortable enough in his new persona to discuss foreign policy on a more than ceremonial basis.

Other changes include a sharp increase in discussion of the need to increase national defense and the national defense budget (from 1 in 1981 to 9 in 1982). Reagan didn't often feel the need to explicitly advocate or justify such increases. He was much more likely to keep such discussions implicit and contained within patriotic exhortations (15 such mentions in 1981 and 12 in 1982), talks on arms reductions (only 3 mentions, all in 1982), or in the context of specific situations (6 mentions, all in 1982). The discussion of such situations was dominated by references to the Soviet Union (4 out of the 6 mentions).

During the entire period of 1981–1982, Reagan's rhetoric is

firmly anticommunist. Hard-line anti-Soviet rhetoric comprises eight out of the 29 foreign policy statements in 1981 and nine of the 58 in 1982. Other national enemies that appear in Reagan's rhetoric during 1981–1982 are terrorists (3 mentions), the El Salvadoran rebels (5 mentions), and Libya (3 mentions).

In every case Reagan prepares his audience for action through his rhetoric. As early as his first press conference on January 29, 1981, Reagan made it clear that he advocated a hard-line policy against terrorists, particularly in the Middle East.[42] So it was hardly a surprise when Reagan took action against Libya that summer. By the time action was taken against Libya, the president's justification for that action was already well-known and widely accepted. The action itself fit into our existing understanding of the relationship between the United States and Libya.

The same is true for Reagan's refusal to deal with the Soviet Union and his position on aid to Nicaragua and El Salvador. Before Reagan proposed taking action, he first set a rhetorical stage so that the American people could place that action within the context of an existing interpretation of world affairs. His failure to do this in the Iran/Contra affair cost him dearly.

For the moment, however, the important thing about this rhetoric is that it sets the stage for Reagan's teflon presidency. His success with the domestic budget, his survival of the assassination attempt, his persona, and his humor all contributed to the Reagan image. But that image is grounded in his ability to control the interpretation of events that are important to the American people.

I have argued elsewhere that Reagan's claim to competence is based on his understanding, not of the techniques of leadership nor the requirements of governance, but of America's symbolic role in the world.[43] This is a key factor in his success as president. Reagan continued to understand our symbolic role. He knew our strengths, our weaknesses, our friends, and our enemies.

No matter what the problems caused by Reagan's domestic policies, polls still indicated dramatic support for Reagan personally and for his position on key international actors such as the Soviet Union.[44] This schism was to remain throughout the Reagan presidency, and is a key factor in both the building and the destruction of the teflon presidency.

CONCLUSIONS

This period is characterized by a mixture of political and rhetorical successes and failures. Ronald Reagan ran on a platform of saving the American economy and "bringing America back." Faced with the frustration and difficulties involved in achieving the former, he increasingly turned toward the latter.

Reagan got his budget cuts and also created a recession that made serious inroads into his standing at the polls. He was seen as a political genius on the one hand, and a "rich man's president" on the other. But whatever else can be said about Ronald Reagan, he is neither a stupid nor an unperceptive man. On the contrary, he is a man who has proved himself able to learn and adapt. During this period, Reagan was both learning and adapting. The fruits of this process can be seen in his middle years as president.

NOTES

1. George C. Edwards, III, *The Public Presidency: The Pursuit of Popular Support* (New York: St. Martin's Press, 1983), p. 24.

2. John Orman, "Reagan's Imperial Presidency," (Paper delivered at the Annual Meeting of the American Political Science Association, Chicago, Ill., August 1987).

3. Lou Cannon, *Reagan* (New York: G. P. Putnam's Sons, 1982), p. 381.

4. Lawrence Barrett, *Gambling With History* (New York: Penguin Books, 1984), p. 442.

5. Lester M. Salamon, "The Presidency and Domestic Policy Formation," in *The Illusion of Presidential Government*, eds. Hugh Heclo and Lester M. Salamon (Boulder, Colo.: Westview Press, 1981), p. 199.

6. Thomas P. O'Neill with William Novak, *Man of the House: The Life and Political Memoirs of Speaker Tip O'Neill* (New York: Random House, 1987), p. 344.

7. O'Neill with Novak, *Man of the House*, p. 341.

8. Michael Baruch Grossman and Martha Joynt Kumar, "The Media as Insider and Adversary: The Subtext of White House Reporting during the Reagan and Carter Administrations," (Paper delivered at the Annual Meeting of the Midwest Political Science Association, Chicago, Ill., April 1987).

9. Grossman and Kumar, "Media as Insider," p. 2.

10. Orman, "Imperial Presidency," p. 4.

11. Mark Green and Gail McColl, *There He Goes Again: Ronald Reagan's Reign of Error* (New York: Pantheon Books, 1983), p. 17.

12. Grossman and Kumar, "Media as Insider," p. 18.

13. Cannon, *Reagan*, p. 405.

14. Samuel Kernell, *Going Public: New Strategies for Presidential Leadership* (Washington, D.C.: CQ Press, 1986), p. 116.

15. Richard P. Nathan, "The Reagan Presidency in Domestic Affairs," in *The Reagan Presidency: An Early Assessment*, ed. Fred I. Greenstein (Baltimore: Johns Hopkins University Press, 1983), p. 63.

16. Barrett, *Gambling with History*, p. 474; Cannon, *Reagan*, p. 339.

17. Robert Dalleck, *Ronald Reagan: The Politics of Symbolism* (Cambridge: Harvard University Press, 1984), p. 164.

18. See "Remarks at a White House Reception for Delegates to the National Conference of Teen-Age Republicans," *Public Papers of the President* (hereafter cited as *Public Papers*), June 23, 1981, Washington, D.C.: U.S. Government Printing Office; "Remarks on the Program for Economic Recovery at a White House Reception for Members of the House of Representatives," *Public Papers*, June 23, 1981; and "Remarks on Board the USS Constellation off the Coast of California," *Public Papers*, August 20, 1981.

19. Inclusion on the basis of values was used 62 times in this period. See "Remarks at a White House Luncheon for Members of the Hispanic Community," *Public Papers*, September 16, 1981; "Remarks at a White House Briefing for Hispanic Appointees and Members of the Hispanic Community," *Public Papers*, July 20, 1982; "Remarks at a White House Ceremony Celebrating Hispanic Heritage Week," *Public Papers*, September 15, 1982; "Remarks at a White House Reception for the National Coalition of Hispanic Mental Health and Human Services Organizations," *Public Papers*, September 23, 1982.

20. Exclusion was used 88 times during this period. See "Remarks at an Ohio State Fundraising Reception in Cincinnati, OH," *Public Papers*, November 30, 1981; "Remarks at a Meeting with Editors and Publishers of Trade Magazines," *Public Papers*, September 24, 1982; "Radio Address to the Nation on the Federal Budget and the Western Alliance," *Public Papers*, May 29, 1982.

21. This tactic was used 28 times during this period. See "Remarks at a Question and Answer Session at a White House Briefing for Members of the Association of Independent Television Stations," *Public Papers*, January 27, 1982; "Exchange with Reporters on the Program for Economic Recovery," *Public Papers*, February 19, 1981; "Remarks on the Program for Economic Recovery at a White House Reception for Members of Congress," *Public Papers*, September 29, 1981.

22. Reliance upon first principles was used 19 times during the period. See "Remarks at the Annual National Prayer Breakfast," *Public Papers*, February 4, 1982; "Address Before the Bundestag in Bonn, FRG," *Public Papers*, June 9, 1982; "Remarks at the Annual Convention of the United States Jaycees in San Antonio, TX," *Public Papers*, June 24, 1981.

23. Reagan argued from definition 42 times between 1981–1982. As Richard Weaver points out in his *The Ethics of Rhetoric* (Chicago: Henry Regnery, 1953), argument from definition is a preferred mode of argument among intellectuals on the Right.

24. The tactic of clear choices was used 20 times in this period. See "Radio Address to the Nation on Nuclear Weapons," *Public Papers*, April 17, 1982; "Remarks in New York City at a Reception for Delegates to the State Republican Convention," *Public Papers*, June 17, 1982; "Address to the Nation on the Economy," *Public Papers*, October 13, 1982.

25. Reagan undermines the motives of his opposition 30 times during the period. See "Address Before a Joint Session of the Congress on the Program for Economic Recovery," *Public Papers*, February 18, 1981; "Remarks Announcing the Formation of the Statue of Liberty-Ellis Island Centennial Commission," *Public Papers*, May 18, 1982; "Remarks and a Question and Answer Session with Reporters Following the House of Representatives Vote on the Proposed Constitutional Amendment for a Balanced Federal Budget," *Public Papers*, October 1, 1982.

26. "Remarks at a Republican Fundraising Reception in New York, New York," *Public Papers*, November 6, 1981.

27. "Remarks at the New York City Partnership Luncheon in New York," *Public Papers*, January 14, 1982.

28. "Address Before a Joint Session of the Congress Reporting on the State of the Union," *Public Papers*, January 26, 1982.

29. "Remarks at a White House Reception for Representatives of the Business Community," *Public Papers*, September 15, 1981; "Remarks at the 1981 White House Conference on Aging," *Public Papers*, December 1, 1981.

30. "Remarks in Denver, CO, at the Annual Convention of the NAACP," *Public Papers*, June 29, 1981.

31. "Remarks at a White House Luncheon for Governors' Representatives to the Fifty State Project for Women," *Public Papers*, October 7, 1981.

32. "Remarks at the Mid-Winter Congressional City Conference of the National League of Cities," *Public Papers*, March 2, 1981.

33. "Remarks at the Legislative Conference of the National Association of Realtors," *Public Papers*, March 29, 1982.

34. "Great deeds" was used 12 times. See "Inaugural Address," *Public Papers*, January 20, 1981; "Interview with Reporters on Federalism," *Public Papers*, November 19, 1981; "Remarks on Arrival in Berlin," *Public Papers*, June 11, 1982.

35. "Great Men" was used 16 times. See "Address Before a Joint Session of Congress on the Program for Economic Recovery," *Public Papers*, April 28, 1981; "Remarks on Presenting the Medal of Honor to Master Sergeant Roy P. Benavidez," *Public Papers*, February 24, 1981; "Remarks at the Centennial Meeting of the Supreme Council of the Knights of Columbus, Hartford, CT," *Public Papers*, August 3, 1982.

36. "Remarks at a Luncheon of the World Affairs Council of Philadelphia, PA," *Public Papers*, October 15, 1981.

37. I. M. Destler, "The Evolution of Reagan's Foreign Policy," in *The Reagan Presidency: An Early Assessment*, ed. Fred I. Greenstein (Baltimore: Johns Hopkins University Press, 1983), p. 117.

38. Green and McColl, *There He Goes Again*, p. 17.

39. "Remarks on the United States Agricultural Policy to Representatives of Agricultural Publications and Organizations," *Public Papers*, March 22, 1982.

40. Hugh Heclo and Rudolph G. Penner, "Fiscal and Political Strategy in the Reagan Administration," in *The Reagan Presidency: An Early Assessment*, ed. Fred I. Greenstein (Baltimore: Johns Hopkins University Press, 1983), p. 22.

41. Each document may include discussion of several subjects. Each document is counted once. Each subject under discussion is counted as a "mention." The number of "mentions" will thus exceed the number of documents.

42. This stance is one that continues throughout the period and for his entire presidency. See "Remarks on Board the USS Constellation off the Coast of California," *Public Papers*, August 20, 1981; "Interview with Joseph Rice of the Cleveland Plain Dealer," *Public Papers*, November 30, 1981; "The President's News Conference," *Public Papers*, December 17, 1981.

43. Mary E. Stuckey, *Getting Into the Game: The Pre-Presidential Rhetoric of Ronald Reagan* (New York: Praeger, 1989).

44. I. M. Destler, "Reagan and the World: An 'Awesome Stubbornness,' " in *The Reagan Legacy: Promise and Performance*, ed. Charles O. Jones (Chatham, N.J.: Chatham House, 1988), p. 244.

Chapter 3

Consolidation: The Teflon President, 1983–1985

INTRODUCTION

This is the period of the "teflon presidency," when Ronald Reagan's image appeared both durable and unassailable. The focus of the Reagan White House between 1983 and the end of 1985 was on foreign policy, and it was the scenario that Reagan built around foreign affairs issues that provided the basis for his political image.

It was also during this period, however, that the first seeds of the problems Reagan faced later were planted, and the first questions about his leadership ability and style were asked. Even while Reagan's image was apparently at its most invulnerable, the first tiny cracks began to appear in the teflon. This process becomes clearest with reference to both the political context and Reagan's political rhetoric between 1983–1985. The data include a total of 1,049 documents for this period: 363 from 1983, 370 from 1984, and 316 from 1985.

POLITICAL CONTEXT, 1983–1985

This period is characterized by Ronald Reagan's personal and political ascendency. That ascendency was based upon widespread public acceptance of Reagan's interpretation of events.

That acceptance was facilitated by the fact that the majority of events in these years concerned foreign affairs, the arena in which the president has the strongest, clearest, and most credible voice. These events were dominated by the Soviet attack on Korean Air Lines flight 007 (KAL 007), the terrorist attack on the United States Marines stationed in Beirut, the United States' invasion of Grenada, the American bombing of Tripoli, and Reagan's announcement of the Strategic Defense Initiative (SDI).

The 1984 presidential election was, of course, also a key event during this period, and it is significant that the White House strategy called for placing that election in a foreign policy context:

> In June of 1984, Assistant White House Chief of Staff Richard Darman wrote a memorandum on the upcoming campaign in which he captured the essence of Reagan's rhetorical strategy. "Paint Mondale as . . . soft in his defense of freedom, patriotic values, American interests," advised Darman. "Paint Ronald Reagan as the personification of all that is right with or heroized by America. Leave Mondale in a position where an attack on Reagan is tantamount to an attack on America's idealized image of itself— where a vote against Reagan is in some subliminal sense, a vote against mythic AMERICA."[1]

The foreign policy events and construction of events during this period allowed Reagan to do that which most anlaysts agree he does best: to communicate the broad ideological parameters of an event or issue with little regard for the details or the substance of alternative interpretations.[2] The downing of flight KAL 007 provided a perfect opportunity for the airing of Reagan's anti-Sovietism, and the emotional context of the issue ensured that opposition would be limited. In addition, his refusal to retaliate gained him prestige as a "man of restraint."[3]

The downing of KAL 007 was followed by the terrorist attack on the Marines stationed in Lebanon. Reagan's reaction, while less successful from a public relations standpoint, still did him little harm. His ability to communicate the public's anger, outrage, and sorrow was so effective as to nearly mute criticism of the policy that endangered the soldiers in the first place.

More important, however, was the staging of the Grenada invasion. While critics contended that Grenada was "really about

Lebanon,"[4] and complained about White House manipulation of the facts[5] and the exclusion of the media,[6] the American public was overwhelmingly in favor of the invasion, and agreed with Reagan's interpretation of it as an illustration of the United States' return to military and moral strength.[7] The power of this interpretation is clear. Americans were hungry to feel good about themselves again—to feel assured of the moral worth of their collective political endeavors. Ronald Reagan provided that assurance in a believable fashion. But for the interpretation to hold, the reality it is based on must be either solid or so far removed from everyday experience that any false claims cannot be readily ascertained.

The bombing of Tripoli and SDI fit this requirement very well indeed. In the first place, Qadhafi and the Libyans had been discussed frequently—and with strong negative connotations—in the American press.[8] The electorate was thus able to see Libya as "the bad guy," which made it very easy to envision the Americans as "good guys." This was particularly effective given the interpretation offered by the government of the bombing as both retaliatory and preemptive.[9]

The "Star Wars" initiative is an even clearer case. Should it be capable of all its proponents claim, it is the perfect weapon—the perfect basis for foreign policy—for a president like Ronald Reagan. First, it is new, innovative, and likely to change the "bad old ways" of the past. Second, "[i]t also has distinct Reaganesque features: it is optimistic in the extreme, built on faith in American accomplishments, and it looks to the future and a better world in rather imprecise ways that are often shrouded in uncertainty."[10] In addition, it is noncomplex, provides images of expansion and exploration, and supports the American myth of salvation "by a single hero."[11]

All of these elements support Reagan's style and indicate how powerful his rhetoric is in the construction of the teflon presidency. More importantly, however, all of the foreign policy events of 1983–1985 allowed Reagan the time to fit the events into the framework of existing interpretations. There were no rude awakenings, and no ugly interpretive surprises. It is this continuity between event and interpretation that provides the strength of Reagan's rhetoric during this period.

RONALD REAGAN'S RHETORIC, 1983–1985

The rhetoric of this period isn't easily placed in tactical categories as it was during the earlier period. Many of the tactics discussed in the last chapter are continued in this period, but in different contexts. Reagan's presidential rhetoric during this period becomes a bit more refined, and a good deal more formulaic. The same stories and anecdotes reappear over and over; the president answers more and more questions with the same story, frustrating the media, and the perception that Reagan is perhaps getting beyond his job becomes increasingly prevalent. Still, Reagan maintains control of the rhetorical agenda and designs policies that will bolster his image and address his prominent concerns. These policies are dominated by foreign policy matters.

The single clearest thing about Reagan's rhetoric during this period is the preponderance of documents dealing with foreign affairs.[12] As Table 3.1 indicates, this number has risen substantially since 1981.

The second striking thing about this table is the amount of ceremonial/campaign rhetoric offered by the president, even in nonelection years. Reagan's standard ceremonial/campaign rhetoric involves elements of American exceptionalism, discrediting his opposition, usually some degree of anti-Soviet rhetoric or another form of scapegoating, and a healthy dose of Reagan's heroes.[13] Like most campaign rhetoric, it is highly formulaic and repetitive; the same elements recur in a different order and in slightly different contexts. Reagan's formula is clearly one that resonated powerfully within the American culture, for his speeches were well received almost everywhere. The only exception to this is in the slight increase in disruptive protests by 1984. These protests were almost exclusively due to Reagan's policy in Central America.

The slight dip in 1984 is due to the presidential election and Reagan's corresponding emphasis on tax reform and the economy. That, as well as other domestic issues, brought Reagan a

Table 3.1
Content of Reagan's Speeches, 1981–1985

	1981	1982	1983	1984	1985
Foreign	20 (13%)	53 (19%)	78 (21%)	71 (19%)	80 (25%)
Domestic	45 (29%)	84 (30%)	50 (14%)	36 (10%)	24 (8%)
Mixed	15 (10%)	39 (14%)	50 (14%)	49 (13%)	50 (16%)
Cere-monial/Campaign	77 (49%)	102 (37%)	185 (51%)	214 (58%)	162 (51%)
N	157	102	363	370	316

Percentages are presented in parentheses. They represent rounded figures, and may not always equal 100%.

certain amount of trouble throughout this period as well as throughout his presidency. When speaking on the domestic agenda, Reagan was frequently on the defensive, responding to questions or charges that he lacked compassion;[14] failed to understand the impact his policies were having on the poor; or was actively working against the interests of blacks, women, or other minorities.[15]

It is by no means my argument that domestic policy disappears from Reagan's rhetoric or from his agenda. It is my argument that because of the competing voices inherent in domestic politics, Ronald Reagan placed increasing emphasis on foreign policy throughout his term in office, and that that emphasis laid the groundwork for the teflon presidency. It is clear from Table 3.1 that the emphasis is there; it now needs to be shown that the nature of the rhetoric made the teflon presidency possible. This is best seen with reference to both domestic and foreign policy matters.

Reagan on the Defensive: Domestic Policy

The single most difficult issue for Reagan in this regard arose in late 1984 and continued throughout 1985. It is the issue of his competence to govern. Charges that he was "disengaged," a prisoner of Nancy and/or Donald Regan, or simply incompetent were prevalent during the latter part of the period, and despite his (understandable) indignation, Reagan never convincingly laid them to rest.[16] The fact that the issue had surfaced more than a year before the Iran/Contra revelations made those revelations both more believable and more damaging than they would otherwise have been.

In handling this defensive rhetoric, Reagan relied on the tactics discussed in the last chapter, primarily attempting to discredit his opposition, and almost invariably treating those who disagreed with him as politically motivated and beneath contempt.[17] The problem with this is two-fold. In the first place, it is not clear that it was a particularly effective tactic, for the questions kept arising. In the second place, this kind of tactic is precisely what democracies need least. Treating opponents with respect and assuming that they are motivated by some concern for justice and/or the national interest may not always be completely accurate, but it does ensure that other voices will be heard and that politics can be conducted with some dignity and openness. The politics of encouraging contempt for your opposition may be quite effective in a narrow partisan sense, but it is not, ultimately, good for the nature of democratic debate. Should this tactic take hold in the post-Reagan years, either the Democrats will be totally discredited, or we will have an increasingly polarized polity, with the two sides becoming increasingly unable to talk to each other and more likely to talk about each other. Neither of these alternatives seems particularly palatable.

It is during this period that Reagan began to use the word "liberal" to equal "irresponsible." In this connection, he also uses "special interests" to equal "Democratic," which in turn equals "liberal" and also "irresponsible." Thus, even when the connection is not explicit, the use of any one of these words implies all of the others. It is not the 1988 campaign run by George Bush that undermined "liberalism" as a legitimate part of American politics; it is the 1984 campaign run by Ronald Reagan. When Bush used the tactic, he was furthering the process as well as subtly underlining his connection to Reagan. But the process began under Reagan. In countering the Democratic insistence on the "fairness issue," he says, for example, that although the Democrats talk about fairness, they "can't see you unless you belong to a special interest group," and continues:

> But let's be fair. This is one area in which all our liberal friends are willing to cut spending. There is one area. They'll cut what America needs to protect her national security. Oh, they say they're for a strong defense. But ask them if we should build the B-1 bomber or the MX missile or the Trident submarine or the cruise missile or the aircraft carriers or the M-1 tank or rebuild the battleship *Iowa*—but that's another story.[18]

Not only are the liberals hypocrites and fools, but they are also working against the national interest. They want to cut U.S. defenses and lead us back to "the days of malaise." This type of innuendo is the precursor to the style of rhetoric that culminated in Pat Buchanan's charge that Congressmen who didn't support the president on Contra aid were actually helping the communists, and in Oliver North's failure to understand that it is possible to disagree with the president—or the entire government—and remain loyal to the country. Those two examples are not aberrations of overzealous aides. They were made possible by the emotional and symbolic agenda set by the president of the United States in his handling of disagreements and dissent.

Another prominent and related tactic is "Congress bashing." In dealing with the Soviet Union, Reagan often used a philosophy of "it isn't us, it's them," blaming Soviet intransigence for everything from the lack of a summit to our problems in Central America.[19] In dealing with the U.S. Congress, Reagan used a very similar tactic. This is particularly true of his relationship with the Democratically controlled House of Representatives. The failures of Reagan's first term, as well as the incomplete successes are: (a) An exaggeration of the liberal media;[20] and (b) the fault of the Democrats in Congress who are against the tax cut, responsible for inflation and high interest rates, and want to weaken our defenses.[21]

This is related to liberal bashing, but it is different and more serious. For when the president seeks to encourage contempt for the opposition party, he is clearly harming our unofficial political processes. But in Congress bashing, he is seeking to undermine the legitimacy of another institution of the U.S. government. Now, few presidents—and no modern presidents—have expressed themselves as completely happy with the politics or the actions of Congress. But disagreeing with them and undermining their right to disagree with the president are two entirely different things. It is Congress' duty to act as a check on the president. Presidents are rarely pleased when Congress exercises this duty. But it is not conducive to greater understanding or to the cooperation our system demands to blame Congress for doing what it is intended to do. Assuming that the duty of the opposition is to oppose, it should also be the duty of the government to take that opposition seriously, and to incorporate compromise into policymaking.

Reagan was very good at such compromise, but instead of treating it as the necessary and valuable foundation for democratic politics, he did it while destroying the good will and respect upon which compromise is based. This makes it all the more difficult for Congress to carry out its tasks, which makes it a better scapegoat for the president and reinforces the whole process. It seems that understanding—and communicating the understanding—that politics is compromise and bargaining would go a long way toward restoring some measure of respect for Congress, which might make doing business with it easier and might reinforce a different cycle of behavior. Whether or not that is feasible, it is clear that the denigration of another governmental institution is not healthy for any institution of the same government.

The only domestic policy during the period where Reagan could take and keep the offensive was in the 1984–1985 discussion of tax reform. Here, Reagan "went public," with a vengeance, giving 37 speeches stressing tax reform in a five-month period, and basing his support for numerous congressional candidates on their support for his tax program. Despite this emphasis on tax reform and the other domestic issues of the period, however, foreign policy remained paramount and foreign policy concerns clearly dominated the agenda. It is to the specifics of Reagan's foreign policy rhetoric that we now turn our attention.

Reagan on the Offensive: Foreign Policy

It was not just the amount of foreign policy versus domestic policy that changed during this period; the nature of that rhetoric also underwent a slight change. This is particularly clear with regard to the Soviet Union. Reagan's anticommunism—and particularly his anti-Sovietism—were strongly evident throughout the period. The downing of Korean Air Lines flight 007, Soviet involvement in Afghanistan, and particularly their influence in Latin America were all fertile areas for Reagan's exercise of rhetoric. Comments such as the following one were not uncommon: "The tendency of some leaders to shut their eyes to the real world, their lack of realism about our foreign adversaries and communism's unrelenting assault on human freedom requires that we face up to the need to restore effective deterrence and help our friends."[22]

This kind of rhetoric accomplishes several things. It makes the stakes seem very high, encouraging support for whatever policy the president is advancing: aid to El Salvador or Nicaragua, or funding for the MX "Peacekeeper," for example. It also helps to undermine the credibility of Reagan's opposition, for they "shut their eyes to the real world." At the same time, it boosts Reagan's credibility, for he appears wise and realistic. He can divine the true nature of the threat, and we can thus trust him to address that threat safely and correctly. Finally, it restates the notion of American exceptionalism; just as communism practices an "unrelenting assault on freedom," the United States and the forces of democracy have the clear duty to protect that freedom. By the end of this kind of a speech, the American duty to protect freedom has become synonymous with supporting the specific policy of the president. It is masterful rhetoric indeed.

The claim that Reagan's policies must be enacted or the results will be disastrous is frequent during this period, occurring in 90 percent of the documents relating to Central America and Contra aid policies. This rhetoric escalated as the controversy over administration policies in Central America increased, and came accompanied by anti-Soviet rhetoric of a particularly virulent kind. The emphasis, however, is not on communism, but on the stakes involved and on the American mission.

It is clear that among the problems the Reagan administration faced in dealing with Central America was the apathy of the American public. Nicaragua seemed far away, and after the experience of Vietnam, there was a public reluctance to get involved in another land war in a distant jungle. Among the tactics that Reagan used to spark American interest was the "Nicaragua is just 120 miles from Hartington, Texas" tactic, or "the communists are closer than you think." When this tactic sparked more ridicule than serious attention, he turned to the "great stakes" tactic, whereby it isn't the people of Central America we need to defend so much as it is ourselves. "Those who struggle for freedom look to America. If we fail them in their hour of need, we fail ourselves as the last, best hope of liberty."[23] This tactic is based on an "us versus them" understanding of the world, where we stand for light and progress and freedom, and the communists stand for darkness and stagnation and oppression.

What is also interesting, however, is that this kind of virulent anticommunism no longer arises during specific discussions about the Soviet Union. Chernenko died in 1985, and Gorbachev succeeded him as premier of the Soviet Union. It became clear that some kind of summit was possible and equally clear that Reagan had no desire to be the first modern president to refuse a summit. When asked directly about the Soviets and our relationship with them, as he often was in late 1984 and 1985, Reagan responded with muted rhetoric: "I think the tensions are, frankly, more evident in rhetoric than they are in actuality. I think that there is less tension today and less threat and danger with the rebuilding than there was earlier when our defenses were so lax that there was a window of vulnerability."[24]

Granted, Reagan had not yet met with Soviet statesmen, he was concerned about his reputation as a "warmonger," and he had to defend his defense budget. Still, for him to claim that tensions are more rhetoric than reality is a surprising move, since it was largely his rhetoric that was perceived as creating the reality of no meetings with the Soviets.

In addition to our relationship with the Soviet Union, other foreign policy issues were important during this period. The most important one in terms of this analysis is the invasion of Grenada, which according to the White House was not an invasion at all, but a "rescue mission." The terminology was clearly very important to Reagan, and he corrected journalists on it whenever he had the opportunity.[25] It is clear why it should be important: An invasion implies that the United States was the aggressor, and a rescue mission implies that someone else was the aggressor, and we did only what we had to in order to protect our citizens. It was equally important for the same reasons that the mission be portrayed as a cooperative one, including other Caribbean nations as well as the United States.

Two other elements of the rhetoric surrounding Grenada are also important. The first is the preparation the American polity had for the invasion. Reagan first mentioned Grenada in a speech before the National Association of Manufacturers on March 10, 1983, in a discussion of Central America and El Salvador. Grenada was not the main topic, neither was it an important subtheme of the speech. It was merely another example of "Castro's control" over the region. It came up again in sundry similar contexts before the actual attack.[26] This is important, because it gave both a justification and a rationale that existed months before the event itself. It is clear that foreign policy initiatives fare better when they are not surprises, or when there is an existing interpretation of events into which a specific action can be placed.

Another important aspect of the Grenada attack is that this marks the first appearance of the "devil figures" that are a major part of Reagan's foreign policy rhetoric during this period. It is clear that all of the trouble caused around the world, and specifically in Central America, is the result of "The Soviets, communist- bloc nations, and surrogates elsewhere [who] rely on a huge apparatus, including the KGB to spy on us and influence public opinion."[27] He adds that:

During my first press conference, nine days after being sworn in as your president, I was asked a question having to do with Soviet intentions. In my answer, I cited their own words—that they have

openly and publicly declared the only morality they recognize is
what will further world communism—that they reserve unto
themselves the right to commit any crime, to lie, to cheat, in order
to attain that. . . . I was charged with being too harsh. . . .[28]

This conspiracy does not just involve the Soviets, and combines the strangest of bedfellows: "A new danger we see in
Central America is the support being given the Sandinistas by
Colonel Qadhafi's Libya, the PLO, and , most recently, the Ay-
atollah Khomeini's Iran."[29] All of the devil figures in Reagan's
lexicon combine to threaten America's security through Central
America. It is thus important that we defend freedom not only
for its own sake, but also for the sake of our American self-
understanding and for security's sake. For our enemies understand the vital importance of the region, and if we do not act,
it may soon be too late.

This is why the issues of Grenada and Lebanon are so inti-
mately connected. It is not sufficient to say that Reagan ordered
the attack on Grenada to replace the Beirut bombings with a
more positive image of the American military effort, although
that was surely part of it. More was involved. One of the other
things connecting the two events is Reagan's understanding of
the world. Remember that anyone who disagrees with Reagan
is either foolish, politically motivated, or evil. In the case of our
foreign adversaries, it is unquestionably a case of evil. They are
united in their opposition to us, and because of this unity, all
actions against the interests of the United States are connected,
perhaps coordinated. They are not above using propaganda,
war, or terrorism to advance their aims. Thus, striking against
"them" in Grenada is exactly the same as striking back against
those who attacked our Marine compound in Beirut. Emotionally
and symbolically, attacking Grenada was identical to attacking
the terrorists in Lebanon.[30]

You know, there was a time when our national security was based
on a standing army within our own borders and shore batteries
of artillery along our coasts, and, of course, a navy to keep the
sealanes open. . . . The world has changed. Today, our national
security can be threatened in faraway places. It's up to all of us

to be aware of the strategic importance of such places and to be able to identify them.[31]

More interestingly, defending the Grenada invasion was tantamount to defending the policy that kept the Marines in Lebanon. Lacking the ability to do anything substantive about terrorism, Reagan stationed the Marines there as a symbolic policy, as if the mere presence of the U.S. military was equivalent to establishing peace in the region. Lebanon and Grenada assume an importance above and beyond their own strategic role. They are important as examples of the scourge of terrorism, and of the United States' response to terrorism.[32] Despite the difficulty of doing anything against terrorists, Ronald Reagan had authorized the attack on Grenada and used it ever after as an example of the restoration of American military strength and moral purpose.

This is most clear in a joke concerning a young Marine pilot that Reagan told frequently and with great relish:

> . . . he said that in every story that he read . . . they said Grenada produces more nutmeg than any other spot on Earth. And he decided it appeared so often, it was a code. And he was going to break that code. . . . He said Grenada does produce more nutmeg than any other spot on Earth. The Soviets and Cubans are trying to take Grenada. He said, "You can't have good eggnog without nutmeg." And he said, "You can't have Christmas without eggnog. So, the Soviets and the Cubans were out to steal Christmas." And his sixth and final point was . . . "We stopped them."[33]

But it isn't only through direct and swift action like the Grenada "rescue attempt" that will restore the United States to preeminence and the world to safety. Despite the coordination and determination of our enemies, the United States can triumph, not by regaining nuclear and military superiority, but by eliminating the concept altogether. The role of the Strategic Defense Initiative cannot be understated in any understanding of Ronald Reagan's foreign policy rhetoric.

Technology Triumphant: Hope through High Tech

The Strategic Defense Initiative (SDI), as discussed earlier, fits in beautifully with the popular understanding of Ronald Reagan: It is based on American ingenuity, it is optimistic, and it is deceptively simple. It also fits in well with Reagan's somewhat melodramatic understanding of world politics. But perhaps the most important aspect of the "hope-through-high-tech" scenario is that it enables Americans to control their own destiny, a theme that is a key aspect of Reagan's political rhetoric.[34] He says, for example, that "Perhaps because we can control our own destiny, we believe deep down inside that working together we can make each year better than the old."[35]

SDI, the Trident submarine, and the Stealth Bomber all have this in common: Through technological innovation, we can bring about world peace and allow the United States to remain in control of its own destiny. This theme arises in domestic politics as well,[36] but it is a much more important element of Reagan's foreign policy rhetoric, where it is important that he maintain the theme that the United States is a force for good in the world, committed to fighting evil and totalitarianism. Progress, and its synonym, science, are on the American side:

> Through the SDI research program, I have called upon the great scientific talents of our country to turn to the cause of strengthening world peace by rendering ballistic missiles impotent and obsolete. I propose to channel our technological prowess toward building a more secure and stable world. And I want to emphasize that in carrying out this research program, the United States seeks neither military superiority nor political advantage.[37]

This is true in his choice of metaphors as well as in his choice of themes: For instance, " . . . the totalitarian world is a tired place held down by the gravity of its own devising. And America is a rocket pushing upward to the stars."[38] Such a use of metaphors strengthens the world view that Reagan is constructing: America is good, America is a rocket, and therefore rockets and technology are good. To protect the goodness of America, we must advance our technology.

Note that it is not our security nor our economy that is emphasized, although Reagan advocates high tech for those reasons as well.[39] But what is really crucial is the tie to the goodness of the United States. That goodness is the element of Reagan's rhetoric that contributed to his popularity, and his inability to maintain the scenario contributed to his loss of that popularity after the Iran/Contra revelations.

CONCLUSIONS

The scenario that Reagan sets up in his foreign policy is simple and very powerful. The United States always has been, and always will be a beacon of freedom and light to the world. We are a special people with a special mission. That mission is to remain a force for good in the world. We remain such a force through our beliefs, our actions, and our policies. There are those in the world who oppose us. They are forces for oppression and evil. We can talk with them, as in the case of the Geneva summit, but only with an eye toward peace, and never blindly trusting them. It is not their words but their actions that we must trust. All of the events and issues of the period were placed into this context. It was the power of the context that helped to make Reagan's interpretations of events so plausible, to his opposition's frustration. The factual truth may have varied from Reagan's interpretation of an event. But the emotional truth was always in accord with it. Because the context Reagan offered suited what Americans wanted to believe about themselves, the interpretations of events that Reagan fit into that context were almost always accepted unquestioningly by the majority of Americans.

This scenario had an added advantage: As long as the American public was entranced by and appreciative of it, they were not likely to look too closely at the actual policies of the Reagan administration. This is clearly an advantage as far as covert activities are concerned, but is also an asset regarding the other policies of the second term. Analysts have noted that the Reagan administration seemed to be a victim of its ideological consistency and early success, for it lacked focus and direction in the second term.[40] There didn't seem to be anything new to add to the agenda, just a continuance of past policies and goals. This scenario enabled the Reagan administration to drift without having to acknowledge the lack of direction, and thus kept Reagan's reputation reasonably protected.

Reagan has thus designed a specific scenario, one that is consistent throughout his foreign policy rhetoric, and one upon which the teflon nature of his presidency was built. As long as that scenario is unchallenged by events, it is stable and safe. But once the integrity of Reagan's scenario is challenged, challenges to his personal integrity and that of his administration are not far behind.

NOTES

1. Paul D. Erickson, *Reagan Speaks: The Making of an American Myth* (New York: New York University Press, 1985), p. 100.

2. Erickson, *Reagan Speaks*, p. 5; Lou Cannon, *Reagan* (New York: G. P. Putnam's Sons, 1982), p. 372.

3. Larry Speakes with Robert Pack, *Speaking Out: Inside the Reagan White House* (New York: Charles Scribner's Sons, 1988), p. 122.

4. Thomas P. O'Neill with William Novak, *Man of the House: The Life and Political Memoirs of Speaker Tip O'Neill* (New York: Random House, 1987), p. 363.

5. John Tebbel and Sarah Miles Watts, *The Press and the Presidency: George Washington to Ronald Reagan* (New York, Oxford: Oxford University Press, 1985), p. 537.

6. John Orman, *Presidential Secrecy and Deception: Beyond the Power to Persuade* (Westport, Conn.: Greenwood Press, 1980), p. 5; Helen Thomas, "Ronald Reagan and the Management of the News," in *The White House Press on the Presidency*, ed. Kenneth W. Thompson (Latham: University Press of America, 1983), pp. 37–38.

7. Speakes, *Speaking Out*, pp. 158–59.

8. Lloyd DeMause, *Reagan's America* (New York: Creative Books, Inc., 1984).

9. Noam Chomsky, *Pirates and Emperors: International Terrorism in the Real World* (New York: Black Rose Books, 1987), pp. 119–28.

10. Sayre Stevens, "The Star Wars Challenge," in *The Reagan Revolution?*, eds. B. B. Kymlicka and Jean V. Matthews (Chicago: Dorsey Press, 1988), p. 176.

11. Garry Wills, *Reagan's America: Innocents at Home* (Garden City, N.Y.: Doubleday, 1985), pp. 358–60.

12. This is substantiated by a content analysis of Reagan's State of the Union addresses during his tenure in office. See Matthew C. Moen, "The Political Agenda of Ronald Reagan: A Content Analysis of the State of the Union Messages," *Presidential Studies Quarterly*, Vol. 18, No. 4 (1988): 775–85.

13. Heroes appear 106 times during the period. See "Remarks at a Luncheon for Community Leaders in Fairbanks, AK," *Public Papers of the President* (hereafter cited as *Public Papers*), May 1, 1984, Washington, D.C.: U.S. Government Printing Office; "Remarks at the Timkin Faircrest Steel Plant in Canton, OH," *Public Papers*, September 26, 1984; and "Remarks at the University of North Carolina," Raleigh, N.C., *Public Papers*, September 5, 1985.

14. This appeared 63 times. See "The President's News Conference," *Public Papers*, January 5, 1983; "Radio Address to the Nation on the Economic Recovery Program," *Public Papers*, January 21, 1984; "Interview with a Group of Senior Executives and Staff Members of the Wall Street Journal," *Public Papers*, February 7, 1985.

15. Women were treated specifically 22 times, Hispanics 30 times, and blacks ten times during the period. See "Remarks and a Question and Answer Session with Elected Republican Women Officials," *Public Papers*, January 13, 1984; "Remarks at a White House Luncheon for the Hispanic Leadership Conference," *Public Papers*, April 17, 1984; "Remarks on Black Colleges Week," *Public Papers*, September 24, 1984.

16. Reagan defended his leadership 29 times, all in late 1984 and 1985. See "Interview with Ann Devroy and Johanna Neuman of USA Today," *Public Papers*, January 17, 1985; "Excerpts from an Interview with Hugh Sidey of Time Magazine," *Public Papers*, July 25, 1985; "Radio Address to the Nation on Foreign Policy," *Public Papers*, September 21, 1985.

17. This tactic was used 221 times between 1983 and 1985. See " Radio Address to the Nation on the First Session of the 98th Congress," *Public Papers*, November 19, 1983; "Remarks at a White House Meeting with Republican Congressmen," *Public Papers*, January 27, 1984; "Remarks at a White House Meeting with Members of the National Newspaper Association," *Public Papers*, March 7, 1985.

18. Such charges against liberals were made 139 times. See "Remarks at an Iowa Caucus Rally in Waterloo, Iowa," *Public Papers*, February 20, 1984; "Remarks to Reporters on White House Budget Proposals," *Public Papers*, March 18, 1983; "Remarks to Brokers and Staff of the New York Stock Exchange, New York, New York," *Public Papers*, March 28, 1985.

19. This tactic was used 72 times during the period. See "Remarks and a Question and Answer Session with Reporters on Domestic and Foreign Policy Issues," *Public Papers*, April 22, 1983; "The President's News Conference," *Public Papers*, April 4, 1984; "Address to the 40th Session of the United Nations General Assembly in New York, New York," *Public Papers*, March 28, 1985.

20. Reagan blames the media 29 times during the period. See "Radio Address to the Nation on Central America," *Public Papers*, April 19, 1984; "Interview with Burl Osborne and Carl Leubsdorf of the Dallas Morning News," *Public Papers*, January 8, 1985; "Remarks at a White House Luncheon for the New Pioneers," *Public Papers*, February 12, 1985.

21. "Remarks at a Republican Congressional Luncheon," *Public Papers*, February 2, 1983; "Interview with the Knight-Ridder News Service on Foreign and Domestic Policy Issues," *Public Papers*, February 13, 1984; "Remarks at a White House Ceremony Marking the Beginning of the Summer Youth Employment Program," *Public Papers*, May 17, 1984.

22. "Radio Address to the Nation on Defense Spending," *Public Papers*, May 18, 1985; See also "Question and Answer Session with High School Students on Domestic and Foreign Policy," *Public Papers*, January 21, 1983; "Remarks at a Conference on Religious Liberty," *Public Papers*, April 16, 1985.

23. The American mission regarding Central America was stressed 72 times. See "Inaugural Address," *Public Papers*, January 21, 1985; "Remarks at the Western Hemisphere Legislative Leaders Forum," *Public Papers*, January 24, 1985; "Radio Address to the Nation on Tax Reform and the Situation in Nicaragua," *Public Papers*, December 14, 1985.

24. Muted anti-Soviet rhetoric occurred 149 times. See "Interview with Steven R. Weisman and Francis X. Clines of the New York *Times* on Foreign and Domestic Issues," *Public Papers*, March 28, 1984; "Interview with Foreign Journalists," *Public Papers*, April 25, 1985; "Interview with Representatives of College Radio Stations," *Public Papers*, September 9, 1985.

25. "Remarks Announcing the Appointment of Donald Rumsfeld as the President's Personal Representative in the Middle East," *Public Papers*, November 3, 1983; "Remarks to American Military Personnel, Cherry Point, NC," *Public Papers*, November 4, 1983; "Remarks at a White House Ceremony for Medical Students and American Military Personnel from Grenada," *Public Papers*, November 7, 1983.

26. Grenada was mentioned before invasion two other times. See "Address to the Nation on Defense and National Security," *Public Papers*, March 23, 1983; "Address Before a Joint Session of the Congress on Central America," *Public Papers*, April 27, 1983.

27. This tactic was used 73 times. See "Radio Address to the Nation on Counterintelligence Activities," *Public Papers*, June 29, 1985; "Remarks at a White House Briefing for Central American Leaders," *Public Papers*, March 25, 1985; "Radio Address to the Nation on the Situation in Central America," *Public Papers*, March 30, 1985.

28. Strong anti-Soviet rhetoric was used 142 times. See "Radio Address to the Nation on American International Broadcasting," *Public Papers*, September 30, 1983; "Interview with Garry Clifford and Patricia Ryan of People Magazine," *Public Papers*, December 6, 1983; "Remarks on Signing the Bill of Rights Day and Human Rights Day and Week Proclamation," *Public Papers*, December 6, 1983.

29. The role of outside forces in Central America was discussed 69 times. See "Remarks at the Western Hemisphere Legislative Leaders Forum," *Public Papers*, January 24, 1985; "Remarks at a White House Briefing for Central American Leaders," *Public Papers*, March 25, 1985; "Remarks at the Annual Convention of the American Bar Association," *Public Papers*, July 8, 1985.

30. This tactic appeared 14 times. See "Interview with Jung-suk Lee of the Korean Broadcasting System on the President's Trip to the Republic of Korea," *Public Papers*, November 7, 1983; "Interview with Bernard Weinraub and Gerald Boyd of the New York Times," *Public Papers*, February 11, 1985; "Remarks and a Question and Answer Session with Regional Editors and Broadcasters," *Public Papers*, March 11, 1985.

31. "Address to the Nation on Events in Lebanon and Grenada," *Public Papers*, October 27, 1983.

32. Grenada and Lebanon were related to terrorism 32 times. See "Remarks and a Question and Answer Session with Elected Republican Women Officials," *Public Papers*, January 13, 1984; "Interview with David Hoffman and Juan Williams of the Washington Post on Foreign and Domestic Issues," *Public Papers*, January 16, 1984; "Written Responses to Questions Submitted by Il Resto del Carlino of Italy," *Public Papers*, March 25, 1985.

33. "Remarks at a Reception for Members of the American Community in Beijing, China," *Public Papers*, April 28, 1984.

34. This kind of American exceptionalism was used 194 times during the period. See "Remarks at Cinco de Mayo Ceremonies in San Antonio, TX," *Public Papers*, May 5, 1983; "Remarks at Fudan University in Shanghai, China," *Public Papers*, April 30, 1984; "Address Before a Joint Session of Congress on the State of the Union," *Public Papers*, February 6, 1985.

35. This kind of American exceptionalism was used 153 times during

the period. See "Remarks at a White House Ceremony Inaugurating the National Endowment for Democracy," *Public Papers*, December 16, 1983; "Remarks at the Alfred E. Smith Memorial Dinner in New York, New York," *Public Papers*, October 16, 1984; "Remarks at a Flag Day Ceremony in Baltimore, MD," *Public Papers*, June 14, 1985.

36. "Address Before a Joint Session of Congress on the State of the Union," *Public Papers*, January 25, 1983.

37. "Foreword Written for a Report on the Strategic Defense Initiative," *Public Papers*, December 28, 1984.

38. "Hope through High Tech" regarding foreign affairs was used 92 times. See "Remarks at a Spirit of America Festival, Decatur, AL," *Public Papers*, July 4, 1984; "Remarks to Private Sector Leaders During a White House Briefing in the MX Missile," *Public Papers*, March 6, 1985; "Remarks to Members of Congress during a White House Briefing on the MX Missile and the Soviet-United States Nuclear and Space Arms Negotiations," *Public Papers*, March 25, 1985.

39. "Hope through High Tech" regarding domestic affairs was used 29 times. See "Address Before a Joint Session of Congress on the State of the Union," *Public Papers*, January 25, 1983; "Remarks and a Question and Answer Session with Students of the Control Data Institute in Pittsburgh, PA," *Public Papers*, April 6, 1983; "Address to the Nation Announcing the Reagan-Bush Candidacies for Reelection," *Public Papers*, January 29, 1984.

40. Jane Mayer and Doyle McManus, *Landslide: The Unmaking of a President, 1984–1988* (Boston: Houghton Mifflin, 1988), p. 23.

Chapter 4

Cracks in the Teflon, 1986–1988

INTRODUCTION

This period was a difficult one for Ronald Reagan, as the foreign policy scenario upon which he had built a seemingly unassailable political image began to unravel, taking the image with it. During this period, Reagan faced a situation where the techniques and tactics he had previously mastered and which had brought him unprecedented political success no longer seemed to deflect any criticism, as the tactics themselves became the focus of attention, and his personal style lost credibility. During this period, Ronald Reagan discovered, as had Jimmy Carter before him, that the task of governing without credibility is a difficult one. The difference is that Reagan was able to recover some of his reputation and rebound to leave office as one of the most popular presidents in history. This chapter details the fall and rise of Ronald Reagan, with reference to both the political context he faced and the rhetorical tactics he employed.[1] The data include 484 total documents: 173 for 1986, 297 for 1987, and 14 for 1988.

THE POLITICAL CONTEXT, 1986–1988

This period was perhaps the most difficult of Reagan's political career. His leadership abilities were questioned, his policies came under attack, and many of his closest aides came under investigation. It was a period marked by scandal, where the down side of being "the Great Delegator" became increasingly apparent. By the end of his presidency, thanks largely to the Intermediate-Range Nuclear Forces (INF) treaty and the nostalgia and euphoria of the 1988 presidential campaign, Reagan had recovered a good deal of his personal standing; but while popular, he had lost much of the authority that he had previously wielded.

Iran/Contra, while the most visible public relations problem of the period, was not the first. As Michael Baruch Grossman and Martha Joynt Kumar indicate, Reagan's problems began after the Iceland summit, with news stories "indicating that the president had been extremely poorly prepared and barely missed being out-maneuvered by the Soviets."[2] This was particularly damaging after the 1984 campaign and the early years of the second term, when the "leadership question" kept arising. In those early days, the questions about Reagan's leadership were not themselves terribly damaging. What they did do, however, was to increase Reagan's vulnerability later. That vulnerability intensified after the Reykjavik, Iceland, summit, and became completely exposed after the Iran/Contra scandal broke: "[F]or the first time, there was real dissonance between who he was thought to be and who he was found to be. Thus, the themes that had been so successful in tying everything together for Reagan . . . turned against him."[3]

Once this vulnerability was exposed, and the teflon began to crack, Reagan became vulnerable to a wide variety of charges. His image, once undermined, itself became a liability, and the president who once could do no wrong seemed suddenly incapable of doing anything right. "After the Democratic takeover of the Senate, the Iran-Contra scandal, two defeats of ideologically-inspired Supreme Court nominees, and the stock market crash, the president's repute was tattered and his latitude limited."[4] The president's policy problems were exacerbated by personnel problems. Donald Regan, Patrick Buchanan, and Ed Meese were increasingly controversial figures, and as attention became focused on the internal politics of the Reagan White

House, it became clear that there were serious problems between "Reagan the president and the Reagan presidency."[5]

The Reagan White House had failed at what had heretofore been its greatest strength: communications strategy and image building. Iran/Contra and subsequent events were not handled with the effectiveness and aplomb of the past: "The media and the public pressed for details and the communication control that had marked his administration was not there. For all the Reagan White House had done in the first four years to 'produce' the news, this four month period in late 1986 and early 1987 threatened to bring it all to a close."[6]

This brings up the question of how people who were so good at managing communications and the media during the first term could become so poor at it during the second. The first and most obvious answer is that the same people were no longer involved. Reagan's "chairman of the board style"[7] was very effective with one staff and all but disastrous with another. Delegation is only effective as long as one is delegating to the proper people.[8] When Reagan placed the same trust in Poindexter, Regan, and Casey that he had in the original Troika, things got steadily worse for him. This is an intuitively attractive theory, but it is only part of the answer.

Another important factor is the nature of the Iran/Contra scandal itself. While it did trap Reagan in the options of appearing either culpable or stupid, nothing in the revelations ever imputed Reagan's motives nor those of his aides. Reagan's image as the committed defender of democracy remained intact throughout. But the most significant feature of the impact of Iran/Contra is Reagan's rhetorical handling of the situation.

As long as public attention remained focused on the Iran side of the equation, Reagan continued to take a political beating on a variety of fronts. But once the hearings began, two things happened. The first is that the situation became increasingly complicated, making it difficult to formulate any coherent and cogent interpretation of events. As things dragged on through the summer, public attention waned. In an environment of limited public concern and attention, the president's power to convincingly interpret events increased.

Secondly, attention became focused on the Contra side of the equation. While Iran remained the key player, Reagan could only be hurt; the facts of the transactions with Iran did not fit into the existing interpretation of Iran as a devil figure. When attention became focused on the Contras, however, the Reagan administration's actions became both more intelligible and more plausible. The facts regarding Nicaragua provided no ugly surprises and no glaring inconsistencies with previous interpretations of events. Neither Reagan's supporters nor his detractors were surprised at the revelations, and nothing contained within those revelations played into Reagan's vulnerabilities. Focusing attention on the destination of the profits from the arms sales instead of on the sales themselves thus became a key part of the White House strategy for rebuilding the president's damaged reputation. The process of how Reagan's reputation came to be tarnished and then repaired is the substance of the following section.

RONALD REAGAN'S RHETORIC, 1986–1989

Reagan's rhetoric during the early months of this period followed the pattern set earlier in his presidency: a stress on ceremonial rhetoric; intolerance for opposition; reliance upon heroes and symbols of national unity; and a thematic rendering of the world in which the United States represents the forces of good, which are engaged in a struggle with the forces of evil. Early in 1986, this theme dominated Reagan's public speech, as the issue of aid to the Nicaraguan Contras resurfaced and Congress faced yet another series of votes on the extent and nature of aid.

Reagan, always sensitive to the public relations aspect of issues, was very concerned with the negative portrayal of the Contras, and took steps to deal with it. These steps involved three strategies: denying the allegations, linking Nicaragua to other issues, and retooling the image of the Contras.

In the first strategy, Reagan simply accuses those who made the allegations of politically motivated propaganda. Reagan first praises his audience for their commitment to freedom and then tells them how that freedom is threatened. Nicaragua is not an isolated example; it is another instance of the dislocation and disease that outside forces bring to a country that only wants to be free. He emphasizes ties between the Palestine Liberation Organization (PLO), Cuba, the Soviet Union, and Nicaragua. They are all tied by one element: communist lies and tricks. Reagan says, "Likewise, we were told that Ho Chi Minh and Pol Pot were nationalists. . . . So today we see an orchestrated attempt to slander the freedom fighters."[9]

Who is doing the orchestration? The answer is provided by knowledge of Reagan's scenario: It is the Soviet Union and/or their well-intentioned but foolish dupes in the United States, the liberals. This tactic is combined with a discussion of the high stakes that are involved in this issue. The Soviets understand the importance of Central America, and because they do, we must also recognize that importance and act.[10]

The point of denying the allegations or of undermining the credibility of those who make them is to strengthen support for Reagan's positon while discrediting any alternatives. This is important given the wealth of alternatives to Contra aid that surfaced during this period. None of the rival peace plans should be taken seriously, for the Sandinistas cannot be trusted to keep their promises.[11] The only peace plan that will work is Reagan's plan, because the only one with a valid understanding of the situation in Central America is Reagan.

In the second strategy, Reagan links support of the Contras to a variety of other issues, such as protection of U.S. national security interests,[12] American values,[13] East-West conflict,[14] and support for the rebels in Afghanistan.[15] This last was Reagan's most prevalent linkage, for the Afghan cause was a popular one, and one in which Soviet intervention was clear. If Reagan could succeed in creating an equivalency between the two situations, he might have had an easier time in gaining definitive support for the Nicaraguan Contras.

The other main connection Reagan sought to make was between the Contras and Grenada, again seeking to unite a popular cause with the more problematic one. In making this linkage, Reagan begins with a discussion of Grenada and their oppression under communism. Then he discusses the improvement since "liberation," stressing "the joy on their faces" as we "helped to restore order and freedom." Then, Reagan shifts the discussion to Nicaragua, where "we hear the same old lies, while the Nicaraguan people see their freedom being stolen away." He concludes by insisting that "we should learn the lesson of Grenada."[16] This lesson is clear: We must stop communist incursion into our hemisphere by negotiation when possible, through force if necessary. Nicaragua, while not the actual equivalent of Grenada, is its moral equivalent. The same tactics used in Grenada are therefore appropriate for Nicaragua.

The third strategy, retooling the image of the Contras, was the most problematic. It began with a reluctance to call them "Contras" at all—a reluctance that increased as the Iran/Contra scandal gained prominence. In June of 1986, he said: "And right now we have not planned for any contingency beyond aiding the Contras because we think that—I've got to stop using that word. That was the Sandinistas' title for them, and I don't like to do anything they're doing. So, the freedom fighters, we believe. . . ."[17]

By calling them "freedom fighters," Reagan is attempting to place the Contras above the sort of criticism that they were encountering. After all, freedom fighters are not the sort of people one expects to be involved in either the drug trade or in human rights violations. And if Reagan can alter the image of the Contras—make them "freedom fighters"—much of that criticism will evaporate or be rendered less credible.

Reagan understood and appreciated the importance of labeling to a degree few other politicians have. He clearly grasped the fact that how we talk about things alters and affects the way we perceive those things, and how we will act upon them. Thus, as the tag "freedom fighters" failed to catch on, and as the Iran/Contra scandal intensified, Reagan styled the Contras the "Nicaraguan Democratic Resistance," in an attempt to restore some dignity to the cause and protect the possibility of aid.[18]

Reagan also attempts to build up the image of the Contras by increasing his invective against the Sandinistas. As previously noted, he compares them to Ho Chi Minh and Pol Pot; he also juxtaposes them to Libya and Qadhafi quite frequently, and a discussion of Libya will often provide the introduction for a further discussion of Nicaragua.[19] This type of rhetoric increased as U.S. antagonism toward Libya also increased, and diminished as Qadhafi took back stage to other devil figures.

This linkage of devil figures is an interesting and effective rhetorical tactic. Once one person or country is established in the prevailing lexicon as a devil figure—a figure whose infamy is beyond question—it becomes possible to place other figures in the same moral position with very little evidence. The same is true for "God figures"; to call the Contras "the moral equivalent of our founding fathers" is to do for them exactly what he accomplished against the Sandinistas. We judge people by the company they keep, even when that company is purely rhetorical. To have had that interpretation of the Contras accepted would have done much to further the cause of Contra aid.

Contra aid was by no means the only problem Reagan faced during this period. The "leadership issue" resurfaced, particularly after the superpower summit in Reykjavik, Iceland, which, according to Larry Speakes, went so poorly from the White House's viewpoint that both "spin control" and a media blitz were called for[20] and acted upon. First, the White House sought to make its interpretation of events in Iceland the definitive one:

> Now, I know it's true that some here in the Capital think the people can't be trusted with such complex matters as foreign policy. But along with the Founding Fathers, I've always believed that the intuitive wisdom of the people is far more dependable over the long run than the temporary insights or parochial pursuits of the Washington experts. And that's why I've said right from the start that the first obligation of democratic leaders is to keep the people informed and seek their support.[21]

This had the effect of preparing people to distrust the other sources of information about events in Iceland. Upon returning from Iceland, the "media blitz" that Larry Speakes mentioned really began. Reagan stressed the proposals that had been made as signs of progress and avoided detailing the lack of actual progress on those proposals. He also emphasized his belief that the progress that had been made was directly attributable to his policy of "keeping the pressure on" the Soviets.[22]

This strategy had only limited effect, however, as the media contradicted this interpretation with one that portrayed the president as inattentive, detached, and tentative. Stories about the president's age and health became prominent, and the "leadership issue" surfaced again. This time, however, the questions were more serious. Partly, this increased seriousness was due to the international arena. It's one thing if the president nods off at a Cabinet meeting. It's quite another if he falls into a Soviet trap at a major summit because of inattention.

Partly, however, the increased seriousness was also due to the fact that it was a recurring issue. If this had been the first time this charge was made against the president, it would probably have been fairly easy to dismiss. But it was not the first time. The question of Reagan's leadership ability had come up as early as 1982, and it had been an important issue in the 1984 campaign. The fact that it had come up before lent additional credence to it this time, and Reagan found few ardent supporters of his leadership style or of his performance in Iceland.

The problems and concerns brought up by the Reykjavik summit were intensified by the Iran/Contra revelations, which began at about the same time. Reagan's first attempt to deal with the Iran/Contra allegations was to deny them by discrediting their source: "I know you've been reading, seeing, and hearing a lot of stories the past several days attributed to Danish sailors, unnamed observers at Italian ports and Spanish harbors, and especially government officials in my administration. Well, now you're going to hear the facts from a White House source, and you know my name."[23]

Having established himself as the most—indeed, the only— credible source, Reagan proceeded to present the facts, which were that "we have had underway a secret diplomatic initiative to Iran," in order to "renew a relationship . . . bring an end to the . . . war between Iran and Iraq . . . to eliminate state-sponsored terrorism and subversion . . . and to effect the safe return of all hostages."[24]

He also emphasized the geographical importance of Iran and the need to protect our national security. The secrecy, according to Reagan, was essential to protect the lives of those involved: "This sensitive undertaking has entailed great risk for those involved. There is no question but that we could never have began [sic] or continued this dialog had the initiative been disclosed earlier. Due to the publicity of the past week, the entire initiative is very much at risk today."[25]

If this last was intended to suppress investigation into the Iran arms deal, it failed. The rhetorical strategy of this first speech failed utterly in protecting the president's credibility and competence. His refusal to admit to mistakes brought his judgement and political savvy equally into question, and his continued emphasis on the position that no laws were broken and no secrecy intended increased the public perception of a cover-up. The public had, after all, heard similar assurances before.[26]

Reagan continued to have difficulty in locating an appropriate strategy to handle the Iran/Contra revelations in early 1987. In January of that year he attempted to displace Iran by altering the agenda to issues of unity and cooperation in the face of the Soviet aggression,[27] and the importance of the defense budget. The Iran affair is in the past, and Reagan seemed to feel that it was time to move on: "But in debating the past, we must not deny ourselves the successes of the future. Let it never be said of this generation of Americans that we became so obsessed with failure that we refused to take risks that could further the cause of peace and freedom in the world."[28]

This serves as both a justification for the Iranian arms deal and a prod to put it all behind us and stop focusing on it to the exclusion of the rest of the Reagan presidency. It might have been an attractive possibility, but it didn't work. Rhetoric can offer an interpretation of an event or situation, but it cannot guarantee that that interpretation will be a plausible or acceptable one. In this case, the environment was imposing too many constraints on Reagan's choices to make the interpretation he offered in the State of the Union viable.

Reagan's next option was to drop the subject altogether. He refused to comment while the various investigations continued and would take no questions regarding those investigations. Instead, he focused on other issues, and made his plea in indirect fashion: "What we accomplished these last 6 years wouldn't have been possible without a solid foundation, painstakingly laid."[29] In other words, "I haven't done such a bad job as president, don't be so eager to condemn me now." Reagan did retain some support, although there was much concern over "what the president knew and when he knew it."

This concern would later pay off for the president, as it became the focus of the attention paid to Iran/Contra. When it became clear that Reagan would not be implicated in this scandal the way that Nixon had been implicated in Watergate, much of the furor evaporated, and the criticisms that were made about Reagan's performance were diminished by the previous expectation of greater involvement.

Still, the problems caused by Iran/Contra continued well into the spring of 1987. Reagan made the first tentative steps toward a recovery in a March 4, 1987 "Address to the Nation," in which he finally implemented a workable strategy regarding the scandal. This strategy had three steps. The first and most important was the recognition that he had made mistakes that affected the entire country: "The power of the presidency is often thought to reside in this Oval Office. Yet it doesn't rest here; it rests with you, the American people, and on your trust."[30] The second step is equally important. More than just affecting the emotional life of the nation, Reagan had denied that the public understanding of the Iranian scandal was the correct one. In this speech, he stops making that denial and admits that the scenario was, in fact, an arms-for-hostages deal: "A few months ago, I told the American people that I had not traded arms for hostages. My heart and my best intentions still tell me that's true, but the evidence tells me it's not. . . . What began as a strategic opening to Iran deteriorated, in its implementation, into trading arms for hostages."[31]

This was an important step, for it involved the recognition that his interpretation of events had lost. Everyone now shared the same understanding of the situation, and communication could begin.

The nature of that communication is equally important. The third step in the recovery of his national reputation is to correct the mistakes that had been made. Reagan promised action in three areas: personnel, national security policy, "and the process for making sure the system works."[32]

The strategy of this speech was an effective one because it involved ensuring that communication could occur by validating the fact that the public no longer trusted him as they once had, by agreeing to an interpretation of events that his audience shared, and by admitting to mistakes and promising to correct them. This was an emotionally satisfying as well as intellectually solid speech. There is a powerful ethic in this country that it is okay to make mistakes as long as we take responsibility for those mistakes, admit to them, and take steps to ensure that similar mistakes will not happen in the future. This is precisely the approach that Reagan took here.

This strategy was not immediately effective, however, for this admission had been a long time coming, and people needed time to let it sink in and believe him. It also took time for the promised reforms to take effect. In addition, Reagan's real up-surge in the polls came only after the affair had dragged on throughout a summer of hearings, and attention became focused on the Nicaraguan side of the equation.

It is important to recognize that attention turned to the Contras because the Reagan White House wanted it there. Reagan, after all, was the one who divulged the linkage between the Iranian arms sales and funding the Nicaraguan freedom fighters, and he often reminded his audiences of this fact.[33] And he was in-sistent upon bringing Nicaragua into the picture. Once there, the White House endeavored to keep Nicaragua prominent.[34]

In the interim, Reagan returned to his 1981 style of hard-line Soviet rhetoric, in an endeavor to deflect remaining attention away from the scandal and onto some common ground.[35] The trade deficit became a hot topic during the spring of 1987, and Reagan, who spoke infrequently, spoke on issues regarding the Soviet Union and Japan rather than Iran. This attempt to control the agenda was not altogether successful, but it seems likely that the strategy helped to minimize further damage to Reagan's image by relying on old familiar approaches and ideas and pro-viding reassurance and stability.[36]

Two other events were of substantial benefit in Reagan's effort to repair his damaged credibility, in that they both offered opportunities for Reagan to go on the offensive with the kind of rhetoric that he is comfortable with and excels at presenting. The first event was the Soviet decision to agree to the negotia-tions that led to the signing of the INF treaty. Not only was a foreign policy success of inestimable value, but this was one for which Reagan could take personal credit and thus regain some credibility.

The second event was the nomination of Robert Bork as Associate Justice of the United States Supreme Court. Despite the fact that the nomination failed, Reagan could still position himself as the statesman above the debate whose policies were attacked by an unworthy, politically motivated opposition. This rhetoric is very reminiscent of that in 1981, and in fact, Reagan's Bork speeches are strikingly similar in structure and tone to the 1981 and 1982 budget speeches.[37]

With all of the success Reagan had in recovering from the Iran/Contra scandal, however, the recovery was far from complete. One element preventing a more complete recovery of the president's image was the presence and public relations technique of General Secretary Mikhail Gorbachev of the Soviet Union. The signing of the INF treaty, and the credit taking that accompanied it did much to restore Reagan's image as a competent actor in the international realm.[38] His emphasis on the belief that the treaty was made possible by the policies he had insisted upon over the last six years also lent him some much-needed stature.

This stature was partially undermined, however, by his partner in negotiations, Mikhail Gorbachev. Gorbachev was popular both in Europe and the United States, and he made it difficult for Reagan to retain credibility based on Soviet bashing. Gorbachev neither looked nor acted like the leader of an "evil empire," and his acceptance of the INF treaty, his public relations skill at the Reykjavik summit, and his intention to pull Soviet troops out of Afghanistan all worked against Ronald Reagan, and forced Reagan to moderate his language toward the Soviet Union or risk appearing as a rigid ideologue. In other words, the demeanor and actions of General Secretary Gorbachev acted as a further environmental constraint upon Reagan, and further limited his choice of rhetorical strategies.

Another element was the continued existence and persistence in power of General Manuel Noriega in Panama. In contrast to Colonel Qadhafi, Noriega defied Reagan and remained untouched by his defiance. The environmental constraints operating in Panama made it impossible for Reagan to solve the

problem of Noriega by any easy method. Reagan tried negoti-
ating Noriega away, but Noriega refused to go; imposing economic sanctions increased media coverage and controversy, but
did little to affect the situation. In addition, a military option
was not politically feasible.

As Reagan's practical inability to alter the situation in Central
America became evident, his rhetoric concerning that situation
intensified. It is probable that the more control a president has
over a situation, the less likely it is he will feel the need to discuss
it in highly evocative terms. On the other hand, the less control
he has, and the more pressure he feels to exert some control,
the more likely it is that he will offer frequent and highly colored
rhetoric on a given subject. To paraphrase a well-known maxim,
"Those who can't do, talk."

The problem with this is that when presidents talk, their
speech is taken as a precursor to action, not as a substitute. This
is largely due to the way presidents talk. Presidential speech
leads the audience to believe that presidential control and presidential action will follow. Presidents rarely speak in order to
convince the audience that they are powerless; so when they
talk, we assume that powerful action will follow. In Reagan's
case, this scenario with reference to Panama could have marked
another serious downturn in his public image but for the presidential campaign.

The campaign of 1988 is largely responsible for Reagan's ability
to leave office with a strong public image. It was a campaign
that focused primarily upon domestic issues, and with a country
at peace and reasonably prosperous, such a focus could only be
good news for the incumbent. In addition, Bush made a serious
effort to become his own man,[39] and Reagan's role in the campaign became purely ceremonial as he traveled the country de-
livering messages of feel-good Americanism and nostalgia.[40]

In sum, this period was a difficult one for Reagan, in which
he lost his teflon coating, and despite the INF treaty and a national campaign, he never regained the momentum and power
that he wielded early in his presidency. He left office a popular,
well-loved, but not highly respected leader, and it is not clear
how history will view the final year of his presidency when the
fog of nostalgia has cleared.

It is interesting in this regard to take note of the reception his "Farewell Address to the Nation" received. In that address, Reagan used much of the same style rhetoric that had contributed to his early success: the "iron triangle" section, which blamed Congress, the bureaucracy, and the media for the failures of his agenda; the cowboy imagery; and the theme of the restoration of American morale. All of these themes were staples in the Reagan rhetoric. Yet after this speech, Reagan was criticized for "petulance," particularly concerning his onslaught against the "iron triangle."[41] It is as if having watched Reagan take on a largely ceremonial role during the campaign and after George Bush's election, people were unwilling to allow him to return to a policy or agenda-setting role, and were uncomfortable with his attempt to do so. Reagan's restoration to a high place in the American political culture was dependent on a ceremonial and symbolic role; any effort to broaden that role jeopardized his restoration.

CONCLUSIONS

Rhetoric is a tool used to establish an interpretation, but it is a tool with limits. Reagan discovered the parameters of those limits in this period as he had never had before. An interpretation, to be plausible, must be able to interact with and explain the world without engendering to many contradictions. Reagan's dilemma during this period was that the outside environment no longer seemed amenable to his existing interpretation. Something had to give; what gave was Reagan's rhetorical dominance over events. From the time of the Iran/Contra revelations, Reagan's image was much more dependent upon external events, which he had only very limited control over, than it had ever been before.

An overview of the tactics Reagan used to establish control, the reasons why he lost control, and his limited success in regaining it, as well as a discussion of the implications of those tactics for our political system, are the basis of the final chapter.

NOTES

1. All of the documents from this period come from the *Weekly Compilation of the Public Papers of the President* (hereafter cited as *Public Papers*). They are cited by date and title. The first 20 days of 1989 are also included in the data; there are 14 documents for the last three weeks of the Reagan presidency, and they are counted as part of 1988.

2. Michael Baruch Grossman and Martha Joynt Kumar, "The Limits of Persuasion: Political Communications in the Reagan and Carter Administrations" (Paper delivered at the Annual Meeting of the American Political Science Association, Chicago, Ill., August 1987), p. 11.

3. Grossman and Kumar, "Limits of Persuasion," p. 12.

4. Bert A. Rockman, "The Style and Organization of the Reagan Presidency," in *The Reagan Legacy: Promise and Performance*, ed. Charles O. Jones (Chatham, N.J.: Chatham House, 1988), p. 26.

5. Rockman, "Style and Organization," p. 19.

6. Thomas C. Griscom, "Presidential Communication: An Essential Leadership Tool," in *The Presidency in Transition*, eds. James P. Pfiffner and R. Gordon Hoxie (New York: The Center for the Study of the Presidency, 1989), p. 340.

7. Nancy Elizabeth Fitch, "The Management Style of Ronald Reagan: Chairman of the Board of the United States of America—Annotated Bibliography" (Monticello, Ill.: Vance Bibliographies, 1982), p. 2.

8. Bill Boyarsky, *Ronald Reagan: His Life and Rise to the Presidency* (New York: Random House, 1981), p. 11.

9. "Remarks at a White House Briefing for a Conference of Presidents of Major American Jewish Organizations," *Public Papers*, March 5, 1986, Washington, D.C.: U.S. Government Printing Office; "Remarks at a White House Briefing for Associated General Contractors of America," *Public Papers*, April 14, 1986.

10. "Remarks at a White House Briefing for Private Sector Supporters of Contra Aid," *Public Papers*, March 14, 1986; "Radio Address to the Nation on Contra Aid," *Public Papers*, March 22, 1986; "Address to the Nation on Aid for the Nicaraguan Democratic Resistance," *Public Papers*, June 24, 1986.

11. Reagan used this tactic 23 times during the period. See "Radio Address to the Nation on National Security," *Public Papers*, May 1, 1986; "Remarks at the Annual Dinner for Strategic International Studies," *Public Papers*, June 9, 1986; "Address Before a Permanent Council of the Organization of American States," *Public Papers*, October 7, 1987.

12. Reagan connected the Contras and national security issues seven times. See "Remarks at a White House Briefing for Budget Interest Groups on the Fiscal Year 1987 Budget," *Public Papers*, January 24, 1986; "Address to the Nation on National Security," *Public Papers*, February 26, 1986; "Remarks at the Annual Convention of the Knights of Columbus," *Public Papers*, Aug. 5, 1986.

13. Reagan stressed the connection between the Contras and American values nine times. See "Remarks to Citizens of St. George, Grenada," *Public Papers*, February 20, 1986; "Address at a Ministerial Meeting of the Association of Southeast Asian Nations," *Public Papers*, May 1, 1986; "Remarks at the Asia-Pacific Council of the United States Chamber of Commerce," *Public Papers*, May 3, 1986.

14. Reagan connected the Contras to East-West conflict six times. See "Responses to Questions Submitted by Noticas de Mexico," *Public Papers*, January 2, 1986; "Remarks to Members of the American Legion," *Public Papers*, July 18, 1986; "Radio Address to the Nation on the Defense Budget," *Public Papers*, August 16, 1986.

15. Reagan connected the Contras to Afghanistan four times. See "Radio Address to the Nation on the Soviet Occupation of Afghanistan," *Public Papers*, December 28, 1985; "Address Before the 41st Session of the General Assembly of the United Nations," *Public Papers*, September 22, 1986; "Remarks to Officials at Reykjavik, Iceland," *Public Papers*, October 14, 1986.

16. "Radio Address to the Nation on Grenada and Nicaragua," *Public Papers*, February 22, 1986; "Remarks at a White House Briefing on Tax Reform/Aid to the Contras," *Public Papers*, June 6, 1986; "Remarks at a White House Luncheon with the Regional Press," *Public Papers*, June 13, 1986.

17. "The President's News Conference," *Public Papers*, June 11, 1986. See also "Remarks at the 100th Annual Convention of the American Newspaper Association, at Ellis Island, NY," *Public Papers*, May 3, 1987; "Radio Address to the Nation on Foreign Issues/ Federal Budget," *Public Papers*, December 19, 1987.

18. Reagan referred to the Contras as the "Nicaraguan Democratic Resistance" for the first time in a "White House Briefing on Aid to the Nicaraguan Democratic Resistance," *Public Papers*, June 16, 1986.

19. Reagan connected Libya and the Contras nine times. See "Radio Address to the Nation on International Violence/ Democratic Values," *Public Papers*, March 29, 1986; "The President's News Conference," *Public Papers*, April 9, 1986; "Interview with Bruce Drake of the New York *Daily News*," *Public Papers*, July 8, 1986.

20. Larry Speakes with Robert Pack, *Speaking Out: Inside the Reagan White House* (New York: Charles Scribner's Sons, 1988), p. 148.

21. "Radio Address to the Nation Announcing the Meeting in Reykjavik, Iceland," *Public Papers*, October 4, 1986.

22. "Address to the Nation on the Meeting with Soviet General Secretary Gorbachev in Reykjavik, Iceland," *Public Papers*, October 13, 1986. See also "Remarks to High School Students Representing the Southern Region, in Baltimore, MD," *Public Papers*, October 15, 1986; "Radio Address to the Nation on United States-Soviet Union Relations," *Public Papers*, November 1, 1986; "Statement on Arms Negotiations," *Public Papers*, November 12, 1986.

23. "Address to the Nation on Iran-United States Relations," *Public Papers*, November 13, 1986.

24. "Address to the Nation on Iran-United States Relations," *Public Papers*, November 13, 1986.

25. "Address to the Nation on Iran-United States Relations," *Public Papers*, November 13, 1986.

26. Reagan made such assurances in 11 public statements. See "The President's News Conference," *Public Papers*, November 19, 1986; "Address to the Nation on Appointing an Independent Counsel to Investigate Arms Sales to Iran," *Public Papers*, December 2, 1986; "Radio Address to the Nation on Iran Arms and Contra Aid Controversy," *Public Papers*, December 6, 1986.

27. "Address Before a Joint Session of Congress on the State of the Union," *Public Papers*, January 27, 1987.

28. "Address Before a Joint Session of Congress on the State of the Union," *Public Papers*, January 27, 1987.

29. "Remarks at a Luncheon of the Conservative Political Action Conference," *Public Papers*, February 20, 1987.

30. "Address to the Nation on the Iran Arms and Contra Aid Controversy," *Public Papers*, March 4, 1987.

31. "Address to the Nation on the Iran Arms and Contra Aid Controversy," *Public Papers*, March 4, 1987.

32. "Address to the Nation on the Iran Arms and Contra Aid Controversy," *Public Papers*, March 4, 1987.

33. He stressed this in 80 percent of his Iran/Contra speeches. See "Address to the Nation on Appointing an Independent Counsel to Investigate Arms Sales to Iran," *Public Papers*, December 2, 1986; "The President's News Conference," *Public Papers*, March 19, 1987; "Statement and a Question and Answer Session with Reporters Representing the Regional News Media," *Public Papers*, May 15, 1987; "Interview

with Television Journalists Representing Nations Participating in the Venice Economic Summit," *Public Papers*, May 27, 1987.

34. Reagan's rhetoric regarding Nicaragua did not change in substance, with anticommunist language playing a key role. The amount of such rhetoric did pick up, however. Reagan gave, on average, at least six speeches on Nicaragua every month during the period. See "Remarks at the 100th Annual Convention of the American Newspaper Publishers Association, Ellis Island, NY," *Public Papers*, May 3, 1987; "Radio Address to the Nation," *Public Papers*, July 8, 1987; "Radio Address to the Nation on Philippines-United States Relations/Nicaragua," *Public Papers*, November 7, 1987.

35. See James N. Rosenau, ed., *Domestic Sources of Foreign Policy* (New York: Free Press, 1967) for a discussion of how presidents use foreign policy to divert attention from troublesome domestic issues.

36. "Statement and a Question and Answer Session with Reporters Representing the Regional News Media," *Public Papers*, May 15, 1987.

37. "Remarks to Law Enforcement Community Leaders Supporting the Nomination of Robert H. Bork to be an Associate Justice of the Supreme Court of the United States of America," *Public Papers*, August 28, 1987; "Remarks at a White House Briefing on the Bork Nomination," *Public Papers*, September 30, 1987; "Informal Exchange with Reporters," *Public Papers*, October 1, 1987.

38. "Remarks to the World Affairs Council of Western Massachusetts, Springfield, MA," *Public Papers*, April 21, 1988; "Radio Address to the Nation on the INF Treaty," *Public Papers*, May 7, 1988; "Remarks to Members of the Royal Institute of International Affairs," *Public Papers*, London U.K., June 3, 1988.

39. Mary E. Stuckey, "What He Says Is What We Get: Political Rhetoric and Presidential Leadership" (Paper delivered at the Annual Meeting of the Southern Political Science Association, Atlanta, November 1987); Mary E. Stuckey, "The Political Rhetoric of the Presidential Transition" (Paper delivered at the Annual Meeting of the Midwest Political Science Association, Chicago, April 1989).

40. "Remarks at a Fundraiser for Former Governor Christopher (Kit) S. Bond, St. Louis, Mo.," *Public Papers*, February 12, 1986; "Remarks at a White House Briefing for Minority Business Owners," *Public Papers*, July 15, 1987; "Remarks at a Republican Party Rally, San Diego, CA," *Public Papers*, October 27, 1988.

41. National Public Radio, "Morning Edition," December 14, 1988; NBC News, December 14, 1988.

Chapter 5

The Great Communicator?

INTRODUCTION

There are many ideas and theories about the nature of Ronald Reagan's popular appeal: that his brand of symbolic politics was designed to appeal to the American middle class;[1] that Reagan "tapped into a powerful need to forget the struggles of the past and present";[2] that "his metaphoric language taps into fads and feelings and beliefs of the average person on a subconscious level";[3] or that he "gives us the past as the present."[4]

All of these hold part of the truth. And all of them point to the importance of public communication as a factor in Reagan's popular and political success. Even more, none of them refer to the policy legacy of the Reagan years, a legacy that it is still too early to fully understand, but one in which the growth of the budget deficit is the clearest component.[5] It is ironic that the one clear policy message consistently contained within Reagan's public speech, the need to reduce government spending, is the single clearest failure of his administration.[6]

Given the importance of rhetoric to the Reagan administration, studies of his rhetoric are crucial if we are to gain an accurate understanding of his administration. This study intends to fulfill the goal of looking at the broad contours of Reagan's presidential rhetoric in order to better understand the specifics of the Reagan years as well as the role of presidential rhetoric in our national life. This chapter therefore provides a review of Reagan's presidential rhetoric and offers some conclusions about the implications that rhetoric has for our understanding of political communication more generally applied.

RONALD REAGAN'S PRESIDENTIAL RHETORIC

1981–1982

During this period, Reagan was learning to be president and applied his experience and previous rhetorical tactics to the task. Some of these tactics, such as discrediting and delegitimizing his opposition, relying upon heroes, and emphasizing values, aided Reagan in accomplishing his political goals. Other tactics, such as his attempts to deflect criticism away from Nancy, his "personal history" response to charges of racism, and his inability to completely control internal dissent (as manifested in his problems with David Stockman), were less successful.

By and large, the Reagan agenda and rhetoric during the first two years of his administration focused on domestic issues. In discussing these issues, Reagan relied almost exclusively on inclusive and exclusive rhetoric. Arguing from definition, Reagan first defined the American community as one constituted by specific values. His opponents were then defined as outside the community of values, as "other," or as "un-American." His supporters, on the other hand, are the mainstays of the American value system. This style of argument is supported by Reagan's use of heroes as exemplars of the American community.

Reagan's foreign policy statements during this period were few and far between, but are significant because of the way in which he used foreign policy themes later in his administration. The dominant theme of Reagan's foreign policy rhetoric during this period is his anticommunism. This is the thread that ties together his discussions on the international economy, Central America, and arms control. During this period Reagan constructed a foreign policy scenario that provided the basis for the "teflon presidency": that foreign policy is a war between good and evil with Ronald Reagan as the judge of who is on which side.

1983–1985

This is the period of the teflon presidency, during which time Ronald Reagan's image seemed durable and unassailable. It is also the period during which seeds were planted that would later cause serious and irreparable damage to Reagan's public image.

The strength of Reagan's image during this period is based upon widespread public acceptance of his interpretation of events, which was facilitated by the fact that the majority of these events concerned foreign policy. The reliance upon foreign policy during this period allowed Reagan to do that which he does best: to communicate the broad ideological parameters of an event or issue with little regard for the details or substance of alternative interpretations.

The Soviet Union was the key international player during this period, although Reagan had few direct dealings with the Soviets. Yet their presence was clear in the downing of flight KAL 007, in the Grenadan "rescue mission," in U.S. problems with Qadhafi and the Libyans, and in the importance of the Strategic Defense Initiative (SDI) as a technology that would ensure peace and end the arms race.

In terms of domestic policy, Reagan was increasingly on the defensive during these years and was occupied with defending himself against charges of being a "rich man's president," lacking in compassion, and being someone who was uninterested in the effects of his budget policies on the poor. The issue of his competence to govern also garnered some attention during this period, although Reagan did defuse the most serious aspects of this charge, and it never seriously endangered his chances for reelection. What it did do, however, was to plant seeds of doubt that would later blossom into a major credibility crisis in the wake of the Iran/Contra scandal.

1986–1988

This period is the most difficult one that Reagan faced during his political career. His policies in both domestic and foreign policy were under attack, his leadership ability was questioned, and he had to attempt leadership with limited credibility. His problems really began after the summit in Reykjavik, and they continued through the Iran/Contra revelations. Both of these issue areas created cracks in his "teflon coating," and once Reagan's vulnerabilities were exposed, he became vulnerable to a wide variety of charges. Once Reagan's image was undermined, the image itself became a liability.

The key to understanding this period is to note that the White House failed at what had been its greatest strength: communications strategy and image building. This failure is due, in large part, to the nature of the crises the president faced. Because the Iranian side of the question was not congruent with the existing public interpretation of the U.S. relationship with Iran, the president could not possibly look credible. Either he lied in setting up the interpretation, or he lied in violating it. There was no other choice.

Once attention became focused on the Nicaraguan side of the equation, however, the outlook improved. Support for the Contras had been one of Reagan's main issues for quite some time, and his actions (as well as those of his aides) were neither terribly surprising nor, to a nation with experience under both Lyndon Johnson and Richard Nixon, terribly shocking.

Reagan's political recovery was facilitated by focusing attention on Nicaragua, but that recovery was not complete. The INF treaty certainly helped to restore Reagan's credibility as an effective world leader, but benefits from the treaty were limited by the magnificent performance of General Secretary Gorbachev and the continued presence of General Manuel Noriega in Panama.

By the end of the period, Reagan's popularity was high, but his ability to influence policy was low. In part, of course, this is simply a truism pertaining to any lame-duck chief executive. In part, however, Reagan's purely ceremonial role during the 1988 general election and after is the natural outgrowth of the type of leadership he always displayed. His rhetoric, as well as his ideology, is much better suited to the hoopla and patriotic fervor of a national campaign than to the day-to-day business of governing.

This last point may well become a truism for all of our national leaders, and presidents in particular. This leads us to the conclusions of this study.

GREAT COMMUNICATION?

Ronald Reagan's presidential rhetoric is useful for a variety of reasons. First, it helps to illuminate certain aspects of the Reagan presidency that are not so clearly seen through another viewpoint. Secondly, as a communicator of superlative skill, Reagan is a model by which other presidents will be judged. It behooves political scientists to understand the model well before making judgements on those who will be compared to that model.

The clearest lesson to be learned from the Reagan rhetorical experience is that effective rhetoric has two components: preparation and saturation. To make a given interpretation effective, a rhetor should begin slowly, with an occasional mention, being careful to provide context for the new interpretation by relying on its connections to an existing interpretation. To make the new interpretation dominant after such preparation, the speaker must then saturate the arena with it.

Reagan's policies and interpretations were much more palatable when they were not surprises. His most effective (i.e., popular) foreign policy actions—the "rescue mission" in Grenada and the Libyan bombing—were, in large part, publicly accepted because the public had been prepared to expect such action. The Libyans, in particular, were clearly portrayed and accepted as villains in the American pantheon, so that attacking them was morally right and easily justifiable.

Reagan's clearest foreign policy disaster, on the other hand, was a disaster largely because the American people had no interpretive framework through which they could render arms sales to Iran as a morally correct action. This naturally caused confusion, which in turn allowed voices other than the president's to have an authoritative chance at interpreting events. If a president's greatest asset is his ability to control the agenda and the public interpretation of that agenda, he must speak loudly and often, and whenever possible, he must be the only one speaking authoritatively.

One thing that this dynamic has led to is the growth of presidential speechmaking. Presidents speak publicly now more than ever before. The problem with this, however, is that "more communication in no way implies better communication."[7] Presidents clearly speak often; it is less clear that they are speaking well, if by well one means that they are communicating important interpretations, facts, and an understanding of the world and U.S. public life.

It is also not clear that presidents are speaking in order to affect change or progress in U.S. public life. They may not even be speaking to justify action or make certain claims intelligible. In fact, in Reagan's case—particularly regarding events such as the attacks on the Marines in Lebanon, terrorism in general, and the case of Noriega—the strength or bellicosity of his rhetoric is in inverse proportion to his ability to control or affect the situation. When a president can affect a situation, he doesn't need to do much talking about it. When he is doing a great deal of talking about a situation, it is then probably the case that he has limited control over that situation. It would perhaps be more honest as well as politically wiser for a president to admit his lack of influence in many arenas. The problem is that the American people seem to prefer promises of action to a display of impotence.[8]

It is also not clear that presidential motives for speechmaking are even as theoretically benign as the endeavor to appear in control. As Lou Cannon says:

Because so many rhetorical demands are placed upon a modern president and because his own psychological needs are no less pronounced than those of any other citizen, presidents often use their speaking opportunities for catharsis, for a kind of auto-therapy. . . . From the president's standpoint, public speaking can therefore be an enormous emotional ally. By choosing his audiences carefully, a chief executive can receive social reinforcement for virtually any sentiment dear to him.[9]

This engenders certain problems in a democratic society that is increasingly dependent upon the president as a source of moral guidance as well as policy initiatives. Democracy is a procedure, a way of doing things, not a system of values. It is a way of making decisions about our moral life; it is not synonymous with that moral life. If it is true that "the real appeal of public officials is what they symbolize rather than what they have done,"[10] then our democracy faces a serious crisis in terms of what it means to be a democracy. A healthy system of public language is by no means the only element vital to a healthy democracy, but it is an important element. "Language, according to Samuel Johnson, is the dress of thought. But politically, it has become, at the best, a costume, and at its worst, a disguise."[11] George Orwell agrees: "the slovenliness of our language makes it easier for us to have foolish thoughts."[12]

Foolish thoughts may often lead to foolish actions. If we cannot trust our language, how can we possibly trust our deeds? And many analysts remind us that, in fact,

> We should distrust language. Ironically, even when our access to information about the country and the world is reaching levels undreamed of by previous generations, so is our susceptibility to persuasion. With more tools of marketing at their disposal than ever before, politicians in the television age can hide almost entirely behind pictures and words, presenting themselves—and us—in whatever costumes and masks various "communication experts" prescribe. This kind of rhetoric threatens to leave us with nothing but the semblance of politics.[13]

This warning is neither new nor directly attributable to the Reagan presidency. In 1975, William Lee Miller warned that

> American democracy is threatened in one direction, as is well known, by absolutists and fanatics who jam the works with their refusal to bend. But American democracy is also threatened in the other direction, as is not quite so well known, by hollowness, by manipulative public relations people and hucksters, by dema-

goguery and the rootless mass that responds to demagoguery, by the parade of hollow men and team players from the White House horrors team, by amoral technicians.[14]

This, of course, points to the increasing importance of the media in our national politics.[15] It is clear that U.S. politics have undergone vast and important changes in "the media age." It is also clear that the full extent and nature of these changes are not yet fully understood. What we do understand is that with the growth of the mass media, new avenues for persuasion and new technologies for manipulation have appeared. Analysts rightly warn us to be aware of these avenues and technologies.

Despite the truth embedded in these warnings, it is not necessarily true that the American people are in fact as gullible and susceptible to persuasion as analysts fear. I find it much more likely that the average voter sees political manipulation for what it is, and that this is one of the reasons for the decline in voter turnout and citizen interest in politics. If Americans desire spectacle, there is always wrestling: The good guys and the bad guys are clearly demarcated, the audience can remain passive, and the consequences of victory or loss are less significant and less frightening. "The contra case, by demonstrating that the continual change in announced U.S. objectives hurt the administration's cause, shows that there are definite limits to the manipulability of presidential argument."[16]

A far more serious problem is that "[a]s presidential governance has assumed the form of a campaign, the White House has added trappings of a campaign organization. . . . As governing becomes campaigning, policy serves rhetoric."[17] This brings us full circle to the question of language and its relationship to politics.

Rhetoric, ideally, should serve policy, although it is doubtful that there was ever a golden age of purely policy-oriented, specific, and meaningful political dialog. Yet, in the days when speechwriters doubled as policy advisers, the connection between policy and the rhetoric may have been much closer. It is certainly likely that policy was supported by rhetoric rather than rhetoric being supported by convenient and therefore ephemeral policies.

What then, can be done to restore a balance between policy and rhetoric, to render our political language, if not honest, then at least more honest? Since it is doubtful that presidential strategies involving "going public" will either cease or reverse themselves, some other solution or palliative must be found.

One such palliative may be to increase the number of authoritative voices able to challenge the president and his interpretations. This is particularly true in foreign policy. Doing so will curtail the power and perhaps the effectiveness of the White House, but it will also curtail the White House's ability to control news and interpretations of the news.

Another palliative may be to simply increase interest and awareness of presidential action. American citizens are already suspicious of the political language of their leaders. If that suspicion could be united with attention and interest, then perhaps we could begin to hold our political leaders accountable in a more fundamental sense than has been the case recently.

The key is that in order to keep our presidents honest, we must also strive to keep presidential rhetoric honest. The only way we can do that is by listening not only to the words, with their high-sounding patriotic appeals, but also to the interpretations that lie beyond the words, and to examine those interpretations with a critical ear. For ultimately, it is those interpretations that constitute the meaning and fiber of our public life, and that finally constitute us as a people. To ignore those interpretations is to ignore the meaning that makes communal life communal.

NOTES

1. Robert Dalleck, *Ronald Reagan: The Politics of Symbolism* (Cambridge, Mass.: Harvard University Press, 1984), p. 64.

2. Dean Alger, "The President, the Bureaucracy, and the People: Discretion in Implementation and the Source of Legitimacy Question" (Paper delivered at the Annual Meeting of the American Political Science Association, New Orleans, La., August 1985).

3. Robert E. Denton, Jr., and Dan F. Hahn, *Presidential Communication: Description and Analysis* (New York: Praeger, 1986), p. 68.

4. Garry Wills, *Reagan's America: Innocents at Home* (Garden City, N.Y.: Doubleday, 1985), p. 375.

5. Bert A. Rockman, "Conclusions: An Imprint but Not a Revolution," in *The Reagan Revolution?*, eds. B. B. Kymlicka and Jean V. Matthews (Chicago: Dorsey, 1988), p. 192.

6. It is also clear that Reagan himself is well aware of this. In his "Farewell Address to the Nation," he discussed the budget problems, and blamed them on the "iron triangle" of the media, special interests, and Congress.

7. Denton and Hahn, *Presidential Communication*, p. 324.

8. The 1980 presidential election is a case in point. See Mary E. Stuckey, *Getting Into the Game: The Pre-Presidential Rhetoric of Ronald Reagan* (New York: Praeger, 1989), Ch. 4.

9. Lou Cannon, *Reagan* (New York: G. P. Putnam's Sons, 1982), p. 195.

10. Denton and Hahn, *Presidential Communication*, p. 55.

11. Denton and Hahn, *Presidential Communication*, p. 324.

12. George Orwell, "Politics and the English Language," in *The Orwell Reader: Fictions, Essays, and Reportage*, ed. George Orwell (Harcourt, Brace, and World, Inc., 1956), p. 355.

13. Paul D. Erickson, *Reagan Speaks: The Making of an American Myth* (New York: New York University Press, 1985), p. 122.

14. William Lee Miller, *Of Thee, Nevertheless, I Sing* (New York: Harcourt, Brace, Jovanovich, 1975), p. 15.

15. Fred I. Greenstein, "Reagan and the Lore of the Modern Presidency: What Have We Learned?," in *The Reagan Presidency: An Early Assessment*, ed. Fred I. Greenstein (Baltimore: Johns Hopkins University Press, 1983), p. 168; Michael Baruch Grossman and Martha Joynt Kumar, "The Limits of Persuasion: Political Communications in the Reagan and Carter Administrations" (Paper delivered at the Annual Meeting of the American Political Science Association, Chicago, Ill., August 1987), p. 1; Dorothy B. James, "Television and the Syntax of Presidential Leadership," *Presidential Studies Quarterly*, Vol. 18, No. 4 (1988):737–39.

16. Stephen A. Borelli, "Change in Presidential Appeals: The Case of Aid to the Contras" (Paper delivered at the Annual Meeting of the Southern Political Science Association, Atlanta, Ga., November 1988), p. 48.

17. Samuel Kernell, *Going Public: New Strategies of Presidential Leadership* (Washington, D.C.: CQ Press, 1986), p. 138.

Epilogue: Rhetoric in the Post-Reagan Era

INTRODUCTION

Having analyzed President Reagan's presidential rhetoric, the next issue is whether or not it matters beyond increasing our understanding of a specific presidency. The answer is that it does. Ronald Reagan's approach to both the presidency and to its rhetoric will have a profound impact on the styles and options of the presidential candidates and presidents who come after him.

Political analysts and pundits are always searching for ways to predict presidential behavior. The one thing that all predictions have in common is their stress on the past history of the candidate in question. While at least one author considers candidates' public language, in the form of campaign promises, significant, no one has analyzed candidates' public speech in an attempt to discover what is important to them in terms of values rather than policy, or vision instead of programs.[1] There is a deep and pervasive conventional wisdom that "all candidates say the same things," and that these "things" can be safely ignored. To a limited extent, this conventional wisdom is undoubtedly correct: Almost all candidates for national public office make their obeisance to patriotism, national unity, and the "American way." But it is also true that each candidate presents these symbols in different ways and that understanding the presentation and reception of these messages is important to an understanding of U.S. national politics.[2]

It is clear, for instance, that both Jimmy Carter and Ronald Reagan shared many of the same campaign themes in 1980. It is also clear that their presentation of those themes was very different. There is little doubt that that difference contributed to Reagan's victory. An analysis of Reagan's prepresidential rhetoric makes it equally clear that certain elements of his presidential style were evident long before the 1980 election.[3] The analysis presented here is based on the notion that what was true for Reagan will be true for other presidential candidates. It also assumes that the rhetoric and style that contributed to Reagan's success will influence the language and behavior of candidates that follow him.

The first section of the chapter is a discussion of Reagan's rhetorical and political legacy. The second section comprises an analysis of the rhetoric of selected presidential candidates. The conclusions elaborate the connections between Ronald Reagan and the 1988 major party candidates and discusses the implications those connections have for U.S. politics and the study of U.S. political science.

THE REAGAN LEGACY

Before we can discuss any candidate in terms of the Reagan legacy, we must first determine what that legacy is. While it is very early to make a definitive statement, scholars have already begun to analyze this question.[4] The Reagan legacy can be divided into two components: the rhetorical or communicative aspect and the political or policy aspect.

In terms of presidential communication, it is quite clear that the "Great Communicator" will be a hard act to follow. Ronald Reagan, as Roderick Hart and others have pointed out, stands at a time in history when not just the quantity but the quality of presidential speechmaking is changing.[5] As Hart says, "[p]residential speechmaking—perhaps presidential communication in general—has now become a tool of barter rather than a means of informing and challenging the citizenry."[6] Because of this, the press, the people, and even the presidents themselves have "lost respect for presidential words."[7] Ronald Reagan is clearly not solely responsible for the demise of meaningful presidential communication. But his skill as an emotional communicator combined with his readiness to continue the trend of replacing presidential thought and action with presidential speech will leave behind him a climate of expectations that include an ability to speak well and the willingness to do so often.

Yet Reagan's rhetorical legacy goes far beyond the ability and willingness to speak. For Ronald Reagan will bequeath to the next president eight years of tremendous success with a specific kind of public speech. As one analyst has noted, Reagan's rhetoric is characterized by simplification, cinematic language, themes involving community, and refutative epideictic, or the tendency to treat criticism of himself or his policies as criticism of the United States.[8] All of these elements place Reagan's critics at a rhetorical disadvantage. They are also noteworthy because they function to impede the rational discussion of issues and the educative possibilities of communication.

Reagan's speech is reflective of trends in presidential rhetoric that increasingly separate policy and rhetoric.[9] Because of Reagan's own managerial and rhetorical preferences, he has accelerated that trend, and added to it the expectation that the president will speak convincingly about the United States' symbolic role in the world and will flatter the country's need for self-congratulation. This "feel-good Americanism" points to the fact that Americans are not culturally interested in hearing difficult truths or negative speeches.[10] They want "a government as good as the American people," which will tell us that "America is back" to stay.

Thus, the rhetorical legacy facing future politicians is one in which difficult problems must be conveyed in simple and emotionally satisfying terms. This task is both difficult and to some extent intellectually dishonest, for the policy legacy facing future presidents will be a complex one, with few clear-cut villains or obvious answers.

Despite the difficulty of assessing the policy legacy of a president who has only recently left office, there is substantial agreement among analysts that the single most important element of the next agenda will be the national economy, specifically the budget and trade deficits. Scholars agree that no matter what the spending priorities of the next president are, the budgetary constraints imposed by the federal deficit will necessitate certain choices. Cuts in the overall level of federal spending and an increase in federal taxes seem inevitable.[11]

Given an electorate that is overwhelmingly in favor of a change in the direction set by Reagan's domestic agenda, budget restrictions are likely to conflict with an increased desire for strong environmental protection, increased opportunities for women and minorities, and increased protection for the economically disadvantaged.[12] Demands for reregulation of some industries (such as the airlines) are likely to increase.[13] All of these cost money. And Americans continue to support a strong defense.[14]

In short, the next president will face an environment in which people remain divided on social issues, support many "liberal" social programs, and are adamant on the need for a strong military defense. Budget and trade deficits and the whole bundle of "economic competitiveness" issues will determine the agenda in an age when Americans seem to want everything but can afford to pay for almost nothing. Given this environment, the political campaign was full of rhetorical pitfalls. The candidates, after eight years of Ronald Reagan, faced an electorate critical of their lack of glamor, of their inability to be Ronald Reagan.

We will now look at the campaign rhetoric of selected political actors from the 1988 presidential election in an endeavor to understand the impact that Ronald Reagan has had on the potential for eloquence in national campaigns. These actors were chosen because they illuminate some aspect of Reagan's legacy. The following discussion is not intended to be a complete analysis of any one political figure.[15]

THE RHETORIC OF THE 1988 PRESIDENTIAL CAMPAIGN

Bruce Babbit

Babbitt brought some interesting rhetorical approaches to his candidacy, none of which seemed, on the face of it, to be terribly effective. Babbitt was the first Democratic candidate to drop out of the race permanently. His appeal was based on identifying himself, and then likening his audience to that image. He is not so much like the audience as they are like him. This is an unusual approach and could have been an effective one. He also stressed morality, and it is the key theme of his domestic affairs speeches. He combined this with scalding attacks on his opposition, a combination that allowed him to claim that he is different from the other candidates.

Babbitt begins many speeches by stating that he is strong and courageous. He is the only candidate of either party who is willing to tell the truth, who is willing to go on the record as saying that we have to raise taxes. Then, "I have a question for you. Do any of you think that we can get at the economic problems of this country without being honest about those deficits? . . . Then I want you to get out of your chair and stand up with me. Right now."[16]

Rhetorically, this is very powerful. Instead of trying to prove his identification with the audience, Babbitt, in a Reagan-like move, is trying to get the audience to illustrate their identification with him. After the audience presumably rises, Babbitt provides some stroking for their courage. He says, "Good. You're right. . . . The difference between you and every single one of my opponents for the Presidency of the United States is that you know how to stand up for the truth."[17]

The audience is put in the position of feeling superior to every other one of the candidates. This is, obviously, a very nice feeling. And Bruce Babbitt gave it to them. Babbitt is also, incidentally, the only candidate the audience does *not* get to feel superior to. They can still look up to him, still feel comfortable that in voting for him they are voting for someone with more courage than they have. A leader. Ronald Reagan used a very similar tactic in his prepresidential rhetoric. The difference is that Reagan had more of a national reputation than did Babbitt, and thus carried more conviction across a broader audience than Babbitt's political position allowed him.

Babbitt and the audience "stand tall" for truth, because they share a common understanding of its importance. Unfortunately, the same cannot be said for the rest of the Democrats.

Less surprisingly, it cannot be said of the Republicans either. "It . . . isn't just a financial deficit. It isn't just a deficit of ideas. It's a moral deficit. It's a deficit of character. It's a deficit of courage. It's a deficit of truth."[18] The message is clear. Babbitt alone understands the depth and consequences of this deficit. He knows how it is hurting ordinary citizens. And, like those citizens, he is outraged. His empathy and understanding of their outrage is both clear and forcefully expressed.

He also relies on the theme of common exclusion from politics. He says, "all of the power and all the rewards are going to speculators and swindlers and wage-cutting executives and de-fense- contracting crooks."[19] In other words, the power structure is skewed. Ordinary, decent, hard-working folk are losing. Bab-bitt's implicit promise is to turn this around, to make the United States the land of promise again. Echoes of Ronald Reagan are faint but clear.

Babbitt's attempt to appear qualified for national office is rather ordinary. He cites facts, figures, and percentages—as do all of the other candidates. He keeps his policy presentation brief and to the point. Babbitt does not make the rhetorical mis-take of losing sight of his emotional points in a welter of detail. That emotional point is very clear: My opponents are out of touch with reality and unwilling to present the truth about things. I understand reality, and will deal with you honestly. I bring new ideas to meet the new realities. It is in "the American national interest to embrace a new kind of competition with the Soviets . . ." and, following a discussion of that new competi-tion, "that may sound pretty obvious, but it has never been the policy of the United States."[20] Negativism is kept to a minimum, and Babbitt thus does not have to deal with a "meanness" issue. Unfortunately, avoiding a direct target for his points puts Babbitt in the position of making vaguely worded charges against the history of U.S. foreign policy. However accurate this analysis may be, American audiences do not listen to it. They prefer scenarios that include a well-defined and easily identifiable vil-lain.[21] Babbitt, in his refusal to provide such a villain, weakens the force of his rhetoric.

In sum, Babbitt uses tactics that are similar to those Reagan uses, but with much less success. This points up the fact that it isn't only what is said, nor even how it is said, but also who says it and under what circumstances that makes speech effective. Babbitt has some tactics and turns of phrase that make for good rhetoric and effective appeals. But in the context of a national campaign, the stature of this particular speaker does not measure up to the quality of the speech he offers.

George Bush

It should not be surprising that Bush's campaign speech incorporates many of the rhetorical elements Reagan used so effectively. Bush, like Reagan, uses a main theme, with subthemes attached to it, all of which are incorporated under the umbrella of values. Bush's main theme is that as a simple but tough "quiet man," he is emblematic of the nation as a whole. He therefore is able to define the values that comprise the American community and define his opponent as outside that community. He uses humor to make his points and deflect the argumnents of the opposition, and maintains a consistently optimistic vision of the United States.

He is tough, but he has compassion. His sentences are short and sharp, and his word choice emphasizes action verbs and words with strong consonants. This structure will convey the image of toughness and help to undermine the belief that Bush is a "wimp." His speeches also contain a reflection on an interpretation of the past. Bush reminds his audience that he has been loyal to Reagan and believes in Reaganism, but states that now is the time for him to become his own man.[22]

It is interesting that he often follows this with the first real reflection of Reagan's rhetoric. He says, "I'll try to be fair to the other side. I'll try to hold my charisma in check."[23] This sort of self-deprecating humor has been one of the hallmarks of Reagan's speech, and it is a remarkably effective technique. Such humor involves taking a well-publicized criticism against the candidate, and making fun of it in such a way that the criticism loses its force and the speaker gets credit for deft rhetoric. In Reagan's case, examples include his famous "there you go again" remark, and his comment that he wouldn't hold Mondale's youth and lack of experience against him when the question of Reagan's age came up during a debate. In Bush's case, using deft rhetoric can help mitigate the blandness charge, and at the same time, such references will serve to reassure people that he is capable of carrying on a Reagan-style campaign.

He will build on his interpretation of the Reagan years, provide continuity with the Reagan legacy, and at the same time, he will prove his toughness and individuality by setting an agenda that is distinct from Reagan's. In so doing, Bush has chosen his issues well. He stands with Reagan on defense and the economy, thus gaining the benefit of the "peace and prosperity" issue. At the same time, he speaks out in favor of a better education system, broader protection of the environment, aid for the disabled, and a strong energy policy, thus benefiting from public dissatisfaction with Reagan as well. Because he establishes a theme of loyalty, Bush is able to use both the continuity and the change themes to his advantage while retaining his credibility.

Another thread that runs through the speech is also reminiscent of Reagan's rhetoric: the continual reference to American values. He defines the entire election as one in which "two different men . . . two very different ideas of the future will be voted on. . . ."[24] For Bush, the difference is between decline and growth, "America as just another nation" or as a "unique nation with a special role in the world"—or between despair and optimism.[25]

Competence, or the ability to lead, is for both Bush and Reagan the quality of faith. Either you believe in the United States that they paint, or you are one of the "others"—not one of the community—and you are also dangerous. Both Reagan and Bush rely on inclusive and exclusive rhetoric: Those included within the community are believers in the American value structure as they understand it. Those outside are people with a different interpretation. Attacks on one member of the community are equivalent to attacks on the community itself.

If one can achieve this rhetorical position, as Reagan could, it gives you rhetorical as well as political advantages, for your opponent is automatically on the defensive and in the position of having to prove his patriotism and qualifications to be included in the community. If that is accomplished by accepting the Reagan/Bush terms of the debate, then the opposition is probably doomed to a "me-too" role. If it is done by attacking Reagan/Bush, the opponent is in the uncomfortable position of attempting to unfrock a priest who has committed no sin.

The most interesting aspect of Bush's campaign rhetoric is that Bush is very definitely his own man. Neither his language nor his themes are derived from Reagan. Bush talks about his understanding of the presidency as a place of "gentle persuasion." He says that he wants to "stand for a new harmony, a new tolerance," and goes on to read the audience a short lecture on the meaning and purpose of prosperity, on the meaning of public service. He says,

> I wonder sometimes if we've forgotten who we are. . . . [W]e weren't saints, but we lived by standards. We celebrated the individual, but we weren't self-centered. . . . [W]e believed in getting ahead, but blind ambition wasn't our way. . . . [W]here is it written that we must act as if we did not care, as if we are not moved? Well I am moved. I want a kinder and gentler nation.[26]

This is interesting because of the tone Bush uses. It can, I suppose, be written off as merely an appeal to those people who consider the Reagan years marked by greed and self-indulgence. But surely such an appeal could be couched in simpler terms, or in the traditional Republican emphasis on jobs and prosperity as the roads to economic advancement for the underprivileged. Bush chose neither route; he decided to speak to the nation's conscience, and in so doing, set the standard by which his administration will inevitably be judged.

Bush may be digging himself a hole here—and one from which it will later be very difficult to extricate himself. One can almost see the protests now: impoverished schoolchildren holding signs that ask if policies affecting them are "kinder and gentler," ditto the homeless and almost any other group. Bush has himself set the standard by which his administration will be judged; when given the opportunity to back away from that standard in the campaign and during the transition, he has refused to do so. The phrase "kinder and gentler" was in his inaugural. It is a phrase that may come back to haunt him, for the experience of the Reagan years tells us that the "thousand points of light" cannot be relied upon to produce a "kinder, gentler nation," and now the president himself has taken on the responsibility to do just that. In these days of budget deficits and their companion, budget restrictions, it is not clear how Bush can live up to that responsibility.[27]

In sum, Bush faced the task of providing an optimistic and positive interpretation of the Reagan legacy, of speaking well enough to avoid disgracing himself, and to make a clear distinction between himself and the president. Bush has accomplished these ends and in so doing set the stage for his own presidency.

Michael S. Dukakis

For a man who has publicly and frequently said that he does not want to be known as the "Great Communicator," Michael Dukakis clearly spends quite a bit of time on his speeches. They are the most elegantly and carefully crafted of all the 1988 Democratic presidential contenders, and exhibit the most similarity across issues. Dukakis places most of his emphasis on the Democratic tradition. Placing himself within that tradition is the dominant theme of all of his speeches. Dukakis' goal is to first restore the credibility of the Democratic tradition and then, by placing himself inside of it, to position himself as the most viable Democratic candidate. Because of this theme, Dukakis relies on the themes of cooperation, partnership, and inclusive rhetoric to project an image that the voters can trust.

Dukakis uses the theme of a strong Democratic Party to provide a base. The Democrats speak to the nation. As a loyal Democrat, indeed as the ultimate Democrat, Dukakis can therefore identify with the nation. In order to establish this theme, he uses the imagery Governor Mario Cuomo of New York used at the Democratic National Convention in 1984. Dukakis wants to "build on Governor Cuomo's theme," and "work together" to solve the various ills of the nation. Dukakis agrees with Cuomo's plans and positions, and as the son of immigrant parents, he understands the need for them.[28]

It is this theme that is most widely known and widely ridiculed by the national press. Dukakis uses it to great rhetorical advantage. He can identify himself with the growing nation and the immigrant experience, which are powerful symbols in our national ideology. Then, based on that identification, Dukakis is in a unique position to know how we have been led astray, not only because he speaks for the nation, but also because symbolically he is representative of the immigrant poor of this nation.

He equates Ronald Reagan with Richard Nixon, and makes it clear that Republicans are responsible for the Wall Street crash and that it was "a government-made disaster."[29] In discussing the economy, Dukakis says, "over the past seven years . . . we've had limping growth and mountainous borrowing from abroad. . . ."[30] It is not those in power who have been hurt by this, either, but "millions of Americans worried about their investments, retired people uncertain about their ability to survive . . . working men and women . . . prospective car and home buyers. . . ."[31] In other words, it's us. And only Michael Dukakis really understands what that means.

Given Dukakis' theme of restoring the Democratic Party to national respectability, it is not surprising that he stresses that theme. This is different from Reagan's thematic approach to partisan politics. Reagan asserted that he understood America's symbolic role in world affairs. Dukakis claims merely to understand the historical lessons of the past and to be able to bring the value of those lessons into politics today. The main lesson, for Dukakis, is inclusion. And Dukakis is qualified because he understands the power of that inclusion. He speaks of his own experience as the son of immigrant parents, of the lessons he learned from the opportunities he was given. He then translates those personal lessons into national lessons. He does not speak in Reagan's such encompassing phrases, but simply and quietly. His phrases and sentences carry the impression of deep conviction, quietly spoken. His language is not black and white, there are no clear statements of opposition. Instead there is an insistence that the politics of inclusion is the only moral choice that can be made given Dukakis' and the country's history. This is nicely done, as it requires a light touch so as not to be overplayed and overdramatized. It is not easy to remain humble and compare your personal life with that of a nation, but humble people seldom run for the U.S. presidency.

In sum, it is clear that for Dukakis, unity and cooperation comprise the soul of his public speech. Divisiveness, in any form, would seriously detract from the image he is trying to present. The problem is that running as the candidate of unity as the standard bearer of a philosophically divided and demoralized party presented too many clear conflicts between the speech and perceived reality for the rhetoric to be effective.

Richard A. Gephardt

Gephardt is the weakest of the Democratic contenders from a rhetorical point of view. While he uses the themes that were successful for Ronald Reagan and some of the other Democrats, Gephardt fails to provide a symbolic context for his themes. He discusses American principles, as did Reagan, but he makes the mistake of discussing them openly, with no subtlety, and without giving the listener a hook on which to hang his references to American ideals. He himself says that, "I'm offering real solutions to real problems—not fancy gimmicks, not mere rhetoric, not Constitutional Amendments and not miracle cures."[32] Unfortunately, this is not the stuff great political speeches are made of.

Gephardt also pushes his message of "unfair trade" in a detailed and uninspiring manner. People in Iowa responded to the emotional message behind the famous Hyundai commercial. They do not respond to an in-depth discussion of tariff policies. And they did not respond to Gephardt's rhetoric. Gephardt made an effort to position himself as honest and nonpolitical, but at the same time he was quite aggressive, saying that the other candidates had been "running for political cover" and questioning the motivations behind their candidacies.[33] This attacking stance can draw an audience's attention, but in the long run is more likely to increase voter disaffection with all of the candidates than bring them to trust the attacker. People will listen to the negative message, and it may well serve to alienate them from other candidates. But Gephardt does not follow this negativism with the kind of appeal that is likely to attach the audience to him.

Gephardt seeks to establish identification with the audience based on the emotional point that he understands their problems. He knows what unfair trade and the policies of the Reagan administration are doing to the lives of the audience. He says, for example, that "everyone from the farmer to the banker to the implement dealer will tell you that . . ." and "every farmer knows. . . ."[34] He knows what they know because he thinks like they do. The problem is that saying this is simply not enough. Persuasion is more than rhetoric. In Gephardt's case, the speeches read as if he were speaking formulas without any sense of their meaning, or without meaning any of it.

When Gephardt speaks of farm foreclosures and unemployment, one does not get a sense of emotional power or truth from the speeches, the way one does by reading the speeches of Ronald Reagan. He does place himself inside the Democratic tradition as a member of a compassionate and dedicated party. He quotes Franklin Roosevelt and John Kennedy, and cites Harry Truman as an example of a president whose policies he would follow. But he does not support these references with rhetoric that follows either the grandeur, cadence, or appeal of these men. As a result, the references lose much of their potential power.

Gephardt also does not make the most of his qualifications. He attempts to illustrate his qualifications based on detailed discussions of his proposed legislation, of his plans for farm economies, and of policy proposals. He is qualified because he knows what we need to do, and he knows how he intends to do it. This is much the same thing that political analysts have been requesting from candidates for years. The problem is that it simply does not make for inspiring rhetoric. Program analysis is all very well and is an important part of politics. But if it is all a politician presents, the American people will not know how to listen to it, and will not listen to it.

Gephardt also bases his qualifications on his honesty and decisiveness. He says, "I intend to be a President with pride in American principles—one who follows them in deeds as well as in words."[35] He believes these values are "worth fighting and dying for" and that they are also "worthy guides for foreign policy." Yet again, he follows this with rhetoric that is meant to be stirring, and instead is only banal: "We have contributed to important changes. Now we can and must do more."[36]

In sum, Gephardt presents himself as an honest decisive thinker, who is not afraid to stand up for what he believes in. He bases his rhetoric on tried and true political formulas, and includes no real twists or passion that could serve to stir the audience. He says what we expect a politician to say. But he fails to say it in such a way that would keep an audience awake until the end of a speech.

Albert Gore, Jr.

Al Gore's rhetoric is much more interesting than that of Gephardt. He portrays himself as a loyal party man to whom consensus is vital, an heir to the proud Democratic tradition and a strong leader. Were one to design a platform for a man running for vice president, it would closely resemble Gore's.

Gore places strong reliance on emotional language and issues. He uses language like the following: "Who says we can't beat a Republican whose first original thought since voodoo economics is to wish American auto workers could match the skills of Soviet tank mechanics? Who says we should be afraid to campaign against a Republican whose idea of self-control is to suggest a little three-day war in Nicaragua? Who says. . . ."[37]

He uses short sentences, with forceful words, where the impact is felt immediately. None of Gephardt's long compound sentences are here. Gore's sentence structure is short, tense, and packed. He conveys empathy through such sentence structure as well as through the content of the sentences.

Gore is qualified for leadership because he is young. He combines "youthful energy with innovation." He says, "Twenty-seven years ago, America left behind eight years of Republican indifference and drift for a bold young Democratic leader with new frontiers to cross. Less than one year from now, America will once again have the chance to abandon business as usual for a new tradition of leadership and strength."[38]

Not surprisingly, Gore does not go into specifics on what that new tradition entails, other than the same thing that Kennedy promised. Short on substance as this appeal clearly is, it is effective rhetoric, for it calls up imagery that can support Gore's claim to leadership. In using this imagery, Gore's cadence is also reminiscent of Kennedy's speeches, as are the images he chooses: high stakes; children; words such as emerging, growing, etc., which were all favored by Kennedy. Thus, while Gore cannot elaborate any specific tie to Kennedy's legacy, and does not even tell us what that legacy entails, he does establish a rhetorical and symbolic tie that is very effective. What is interesting is that in his discussion of the Soviet Union, Gore does not make any comparisons between himself and John F. Kennedy; perhaps he feels that Kennedy's record in that area had best be ignored.

Part of what makes Gore's rhetoric so effective is his low-key approach. He makes it very clear that in identifying himself with Kennedy he is supporting not only his own position, but also that of the Democratic Party. Reagan's success with the "Eleventh Commandment" has clearly inspired the Democrats. One of Gore's approaches to establishing himself as a "company man" is to discuss the myths that Ronald Reagan would have us believe about the Democrats: They will halt national defense spending, they will become less compassionate, and they will raise taxes for midincome Americans. Gore explodes these myths, not only for himself, but also for the Democratic Party as a whole.

In sum, Gore relies on sharp, tightly worded rhetoric to establish his claim to the Kennedy legacy and to the U.S. presidency. He does not appear sharp enough nor focused enough to be serious about running for the presidency. His speech lacks the edge that the other candidates display. Yet Gore is well positioned for the vice presidency—as a strong party man and the only Southerner in the race, the thought must have crossed his mind—and it has clearly occurred to his speechwriters.

Gary Hart

Gary Hart is perhaps the most interesting of all the candidates from a rhetorical perspective. His rhetoric, more than any of the other candidates', resembles that of Ronald Reagan. The degree of similarity in their speech patterns is remarkable and may go a long way in explaining Hart's initial popularity. People were responding to the same thing in Hart that they responded to in Reagan. Specifically, Hart's claim to presidential qualification is two-fold: He understands America's symbolic role in the world, and he has plans and ideas for actualizing that role. He also uses back-handed tactics to discredit his opposition, argues by reference to authority, and speaks to American values. While Reagan and Hart offer very different understandings of U.S. politics, they express themselves in nearly identical fashion.

First, Hart claims to understand the United States' symbolic role in the world. In elaborating this interpretation, he, like Reagan, uses the tactic of definition through opposition. Indeed, as far as Hart is concerned, there are no opponents except Reagan. He is explicitly running against Reagan and Reaganism. He says, "our nation is drifting backwards over the waterfall of history. . . . [M]arkets do not provide milk to babies living in poverty. . . ."[39] These words could have come from Reagan, although "markets" would have been "government programs."

Hart also inverts Reagan symbolically. He calls his domestic program "SII" or Strategic Investment Initiative, and explicitly contrasts it to Reagan's "SDI" or Strategic Defense Initiative. In so doing, Hart offers a new interpretation of the role of government, just as Reagan offered his interpretation. He goes on to charge Reagan with dishonesty, and at the same time uses Reaganesque rhetoric to discredit the president. He says, "Although their findings have been ignored by the current Administration, the needs are clear."[40] Reagan was saying the same things about Carter in 1980.

Like Reagan, Hart claims to know the needs of the future and is therefore in a position to direct the United States toward that future. Also like Reagan, Hart relies on the notion of new leadership to establish his qualification. He says, "We need leadership willing to talk the straightforward truth about our country's problems, and courageous enough to propose concrete programs to solve the problems we've got."[41] He ends this particular speech with a lengthy quote from Robert Kennedy, providing a source of support for his argument that few Democrats will quarrel with.

He also uses Reagan's tactic of discrediting the opposition by rendering their motives dubious if not unpatriotic. People who disagree with Reagan are either misinformed or communists. People who disagree with Hart are either misinformed or lacking in compassion. Hart, like Reagan, believes in "democracy and opportunity"; like Reagan, he sees a Congress that "reacts with bluster and no action." Unlike Reagan, however, his opponents are not Soviet sympathizers (monsters); they are wealthy Republicans (monsters). He says, "We must prove to the world that we can reintroduce a sense of national responsibility."[42] Who lost us that sense? Why, the Republicans, of course. The rhetoric here is reminiscent of Reagan's challenges to Brown in the 1960s and to Ford and Carter in the 1970s.

In sum, Hart portrays himself as strong, cooperative, understanding, and compassionate. Those who disagree with him are opposite to him and are therefore weak, uncooperative, lacking in understanding, and noncompassionate. This kind of rhetoric is effective and emotionally satisfying. Both Hart and Reagan are skilled at its use. These similarities were clearly part of what made Hart the Democratic front-runner. Unfortunately for him, communication and rhetoric are not the only important aspects of any campaign.

Jesse Jackson

Jackson's rhetoric is problematic because his speech tends to be improvised. While his staff says that the content of the transcripts are faithful reproductions of Jackson's beliefs, they may not be faithful representations of his presentation of those beliefs. Since this study focuses on image more than content, this is a potential problem.

In general, Jackson's speeches show strong thematic unity. There are no significant differences in his approaches to foreign and domestic affairs. He stresses the commonality of goals between himself and his audience. It is on this point that he clearly hopes to build and maintain the "Rainbow Coalition." He speaks forcefully and emotionally of the moral outrage his audience must be feeling at the various injustices of American society. He emphasizes that his fitness for national office is based on his strong moral convictions and knowledge of events.

There is some evidence that Jackson's appeal is much broader than many analysts initially expected.[43] This analysis suggests that his rhetoric contributed to the breadth of his appeal. Jackson stresses the importance of common goals. These goals are economic. He may not eat Wisconsin cheese on the campaign trail, but he stands with Wisconsin workers on the picket line. He says that "[i]nvesting in America means an economic policy that invests in people—as workers, as students, as homebuyers, and as farmers."[44] All of these groups are economic groups, and it is their shared economic interests that Jackson stresses.

He also relies heavily on the theme of shared outrage, a theme he shares with Ronald Reagan, although the two are clearly outraged by different perceptions of injustice. He speaks at great length on the problem of a rich land whose people are poor. He says:

> Who knows better than you who have watched our most beautiful cities decay at the core the major infrastructure needs? You, who see the unemployment lines swollen with a generation who has never known steady work and those who were once productive industrial workers, know the training needs! And you, who have watched the closed signs go up on plant gates and shop fronts as industry and the businesses that depend on it abandon your communities, know the importance of reindustrializing the economy.[45]

An important element in this passage is that it is inclusive. Jackson is not appealing only to those who have stood in a welfare line, but to all those who have seen it, or heard of it, and who want to put an end to poverty. In addition, Jackson's message, while evocative of the problems of the urban North, is not only negative. This is important, because of the dangers inherent in negative appeals: You may detach people from whatever you are opposing, but that does not ensure that they will therefore be attached to you. Jackson provides a measure of that assurance by pounding home a positive message as strongly as he stresses the outrage of the negative message. "You see these problems, you are moved by them, and you can do something about them." This is very effective rhetoric, because at the same time that Jackson is describing the ills of modern America, he is also saying that they can be changed, and changed by his audience. This gives the audience a strong message of hope and empowerment, which may be one of the keys to Jackson's success among the economically and politically disenfranchised.

As a minister, Jackson can speak with a moral force unique among the Democrats. When this moral force is combined with a powerful sense of outrage, it makes for excellent rhetoric. He says, "I . . . have strong convictions about a proper role for the United States in world affairs. This role must have a proper moral context and underpinning. . . ."[46] Other candidates promise to be honest with the voters, or to maintain honest government; the implication is that they will also have moral government. Jackson stands alone in promising not morality through the use of government, but moral government. It is different, and it is an effective appeal.

Jackson is also quick to stress his detailed knowledge of events. He discusses developments within and among African states, detailed plans for urban renewal, and a new economic program with confidence and ease. This is not all that unusual among candidates. What is unusual, at least among the candidates represented here, is that Jackson places this knowledge within a context. Unlike Reagan or Hart, it is not a purely symbolic context. It is the context of internationalism. Because the infrastructure is one of Jackson's major concerns, it is easy for him to tie the economic problems of U.S. cities to the economies of the Third World, to connect American racism with South African apartheid, and to understand U.S. foreign policy within the context of debtor nations. This is not pure symbolism, which simplifies the world for the audience. It is an attempt to get the audience to see the world as a complex interrelated web of relationships and that no one part of that web can be understood in isolation from the rest. Part of Jackson's claim to competence is the claim that he understands that the web exists and that issues must be seen as part of it.

In sum, Jackson uses very effective rhetorical techniques to communicate the elements of trust. His rhetoric is stirring and powerful. He includes detailed and specific policy proposals and programs and, by communicating his view of the world, is making an attempt to both influence and educate the American people. He is also adept at using appeals to emotion and may forsake education for debate points. It is here that his spoken rhetoric may differ from his written speeches, and it is precisely this important point that this analysis is incapable of resolving.

CONCLUSIONS

This study has revealed both similarities and differences among presidential candidates. It is clear, for instance, that some tactics are common to the genus "politician." All candidates during a primary emphasize party loyalty. All candidates base their qualification, in part, on claims that "I know what the country ought to do, and I have plans to get there," although there is variation in how detailed discussions of these plans are. In short, the conventional wisdom that political appeals are based on amorphous and non-controversial statements involving more symbol than substance is borne out by the evidence.

The evidence also indicates things neglected by conventional wisdom, however. Babbitt's rhetoric, for instance, is a good example of the dangers of negative rhetoric. Negativism may detach the audience from something, but to be effective, it must also attach the audience to something. Discrediting your opposition is not enough to reflect credit upon yourself. Babbitt is also reflective of the importance of the speaker's status. When he uses Reagan-style rhetoric, it is with limited success. He does not seem to be able to make the substance of those arguments convincing. The same arguments, coming from Ronald Reagan, who had attained a national reputation, were given much more attention. It is clear that rhetoric involves who is speaking as much as what is being said. From this, it is clear that while other politicians may use the tactics and rhetorical structures of a Kennedy, a Roosevelt, or a Reagan, these tactics and structures alone will not make that candidate a Kennedy, a Roosevelt, or a Reagan.

Gephardt, on the other hand, is a very good example of the importance of providing a symbolic context or theme through which an audience can understand and interpret events. In the absence of such a context, neither the candidate nor his message is intelligible or powerful.

A final observation concerns the nature of the appeals used by the candidates in the study. All of the appeals that are powerful and convincing involve appeals to emotion. This issue has two sides to it: the candidate and the audience. From the perspective of the audience, when our political speech involves emotional appeals and high symbolism, when our orators are expected to entertain rather than enlighten us, we will generate a certain kind of leader. Children learn to watch television at ever-earlier ages; they have developed a decreasing tolerance for things that do not come in tidy, emotionally appealing, and simple packages. Quite simply, people are not learning to listen to substantive rhetoric, and they are paying the price in leadership.

From the perspective of the candidates, when they appeal to reason they become dry and their rhetoric loses much of its force. This is a disturbing development. For in focusing on emotional appeals, political speakers are contributing to a debasement of our political speech and political symbolism. The symbols being used become cheapened; their meanings become less well defined. They are routes to an emotional reaction, and serve as ends in themselves rather than as tools for communicating about substantive and important issues.

The question is really one of the connection between good rhetoric and good politics. Reagan and Hart, for example, are masterful in their use of emotional appeals and evocative symbolism. But what kind of politics does this rhetoric lead us to? Political scientists are increasingly concerned with the question of image over substance in our national politics. Nowhere is this issue more clear than in the rhetoric of the candidates for national office.

NOTES

Portions of this chapter were presented at the Annual Meeting of the American Political Science Association, Washington, D.C., August

1988; at the Annual Meeting of the Southern Political Science Association, Atlanta, Ga., 1988; and at the Midwest Political Science Association, Chicago, Ill., April 1989.

1. Jeff Fishel, *Presidents and Promises* (Washington, D.C.: CQ Press, 1985); Ronald H. Carpenter, et al., "Style in Discourse as a Predictor of Presidential Personality for Mr. Carter and Other Twentieth Century Presidents: Testing the Barber Paradigm," *Presidential Studies Quarterly*, Vol. 8, No. 1 (1978): 67–78.

2. M. Brewster Smith, Jerome Bruner, and Ralph White, *Opinions and Personality* (New York: Wiley, 1964); Ronald Berkman and Laura W. Kitch, *Politics in the Media Age* (New York: McGraw-Hill, 1986); Charles D. Elder and Roger W. Cobb, *The Political Uses of Symbols* (New York: Longman, 1983); Richard L. Rubin, *Press, Party, and the Presidency* (New York, W. W. Norton, 1981).

3. Mary E. Stuckey, *Getting Into the Game: The Pre-Presidential Rhetoric of Ronald Reagan* (New York: Praeger, 1989).

4. B. B. Kymlicka and Jean V. Matthews, eds., *The Reagan Revolution?* (Chicago: Dorsey, 1988); Charles O. Jones, ed., *The Reagan Legacy: Promise and Performance* (Chatham, N.J.: Chatham House, 1988); John L. Palmer and Isabel V. Sawhill, ed., *The Reagan Experiment* (Washington, D.C.: The Urban Institute Press, 1982); and Fred I. Greenstein, *The Reagan Presidency: An Early Assessment* (Baltimore: Johns Hopkins University Press, 1983).

5. Roderick P. Hart, *The Sound of Leadership: Presidential Communication in the Modern Age* (Chicago: University of Chicago Press, 1987); James Ceasar, et al. "The Rise of the Rhetorical Presidency," in *Essays in Presidential Rhetoric*, ed. Theodore Windt and Beth Ingold (Dubuque: Kendall/ Hunt, 1983).

6. Hart, *Sound of Leadership*, p. 212.

7. Hart, *Sound of Leadership*, p. 212.

8. Craig Allen Smith, "Trouble Came to MisteReagan's Neighborhood: Observations on Iran/Contra and the Reagan Rhetoric" (Paper delivered at the Annual Meeting of the American Political Science Association, Washington, D.C., August 1988).

9. Martha Joynt Kumar and Michael Baruch Grossman, "Establishing an Administration: The Role of Communications in the Carter and Reagan Transitions" (Paper delivered at the Annual Meeting of the American Political Science Association, Washington, D.C., August 1988); Charles Walcott and Karen M. Hult, "The Presidential Speechwriting Process: Evolution of an Organizational Function" (Paper delivered at the Annual Meeting of the American Political Science Association, Washington, D.C., August 1988).

10. H. M. Zullow, G. Oettingen, and M.E.P. Seligman, "Pessimistic Explanatory Style in the Historical Record: Caving LBJ, Presidential candidates, and East versus West Berlin," *American Psychology* (in press); H. M. Zullow and M.E.P. Seligman, "Pessimistic Rumination Predicts Defeat of Presidential Candidates, 1900–1984."

11. James Tobin, "Reaganomics in Retrospect," in *The Reagan Revolution?*, eds. B. B. Kymlicka and J. V. Matthews (Chicago: Dorsey, 1988), pp. 85–104. William A. Niskanen, "Reflections on Reaganomics," in *Reagan Revolution?*, eds. B. B. Kymlicka and J. V. Matthews, pp. 104–10; Paul E. Peterson and Mark Rom, "Lower Taxes, More Spending, and Budget Deficits," in *The Reagan Legacy*, ed. Charles O. Jones, pp. 213–40.

12. Lou Harris Poll, National Public Radio, "Morning Edition," September 12, 1988.

13. *Gallup Report*, November, 1987, pp. 30–31.

14. *Gallup Report* (Princeton, N.J.: The Gallup Poll, November, 1987), pp. 8–9.

15. The data for all political actors were obtained from their campaign headquarters.

16. Governor Babbitt's Campaign Appearances, January 4–8, 1988.

17. Governor Babbitt's Campaign Appearances, January 4–8, 1988.

18. Governor Babbitt's Campaign Appearances, January 4–8, 1988.

19. Governor Babbitt's Campaign Appearances, January 4–8, 1988.

20. Quoted in "Fact Sheet: Rethinking Arms Security," Remarks prepared for delivery at the Fletcher School of Law and Diplomacy, Tufts University, Boston, September 30, 1987.

21. Edgar Crane, *Marketing Communication: A Behavioral Approach to Men, Messages, and Media* (New York: John Wiley and Sons, 1965); John H. Kessel, *Presidential Campaign Politics*, 3d ed. (Chicago: Dorsey Press, 1988); Marthe Anne Martin, "Ideologues, Ideographs, and the 'Best Men': From Carter to Reagan," *Southern Speech Communication Journal* 49 (1983–1984): 12–25; Richard Hofstadter, *The Paranoid Style in American Politics and Other Essays* (New York: Alfred A. Knopf, 1978).

22. "Speech Accepting the Republican Nomination for President of the United States," Legislate, database of *The Washington Post*, Washington, D.C., August 18, 1988.

23. "Speech Accepting the Republican Nomination," Legislate database, August 18, 1988. See also (all in Legislate database) "Address to the National Republican Governor's Conference," Point Clear, Ala., November 22, 1988; "Post-Election Press Conference with Vice President George Bush," Houston, Tex., November 11, 1988.

24. "Speech Accepting the Republican Nomination for President of the United States," Legislate database, August 18, 1988.

25. "Speech Accepting the Republican Nomination," Legislate database, August 18, 1988.

26. "Speech Accepting the Republican Nomination," Legislate database, August 18, 1988.

27. The author is indebted to Lisa Walker for her thoughts on this subject.

28. "An Agenda for Economic Growth," New York City, Legislate database, November 12, 1988.

29. "The Promise of America," Des Moines, Iowa, Legislate database, January 7, 1988.

30. "The Promise of America," Des Moines, Iowa, Legislate database, January 7, 1988.

31. "The Promise of America," Des Moines, Iowa, Legislate database, January 7, 1988.

32. "Remarks," Georgetown University, Washington, D.C., Legislate database, November 11, 1988.

33. "Remarks," Georgetown University, Washington, D.C., Legislate database, November 11, 1988.

34. "The Gephardt Plan for Rural Renewal," Des Moines, Iowa, Legislate database, October 15, 1987.

35. "A New Internationalism: American Foreign Policy in the Years Ahead," Speech before the World Affairs Council, Los Angeles, Calif., Legislate database, August 20, 1987.

36. "New Internationalism," Legislate database, August 20, 1987.

37. "Remarks," National Press Club, Legislate database, October 6, 1988.

38. "Remarks," University of New Hampshire, Legislate database, December 3, 1987.

39. "A Strategic Investment Initiative," State University of New York, Binghamton, N.Y., Legislate database, October 8, 1987.

40. "Strategic Investment Initiative," Legislate database, October 8, 1987.

41. "Strategic Investment Initiative," Legislate database, October 8, 1987.

42. "Enlightened Internationalism," State University of New York, Legislate database, October 6, 1987.

43. "The Big Apple Showdown," *Time Magazine*, April 18, 1988: pp. 22–24.

44. "Invest in America—Rebuild Our Cities," Nashville, Tenn., Legislate database, June 15, 1987.

45. "Invest in America," Legislate database, June 15, 1987.

46. "An American Agenda with South Africa," Transafrica Presidential Forum, Washington, D.C., Legislate database, June 5, 1987.

Selected Bibliography

Alexandre, Laurien. "In the Service of the State: Public Diplomacy, Government, Media, and Ronald Reagan." *Media, Culture, and Society* vol. 1, no. 9 (1987): 29–46.

Alger, Dean. "The President, the Bureaucracy, and the People: Discretion in Implementation and the Source of Legitimacy Question." Paper delivered at the Annual Meeting of the American Political Science Association, New Orleans, La., 1985.

Alter, Jonathan. "Rooting for Reagan." *Washington Monthly* vol. 12, no. 11 (1981): 12–17.

Andrews, James R. *The Practice of Rhetorical Criticism*. New York: Macmillan, 1983.

Arkes, Hadley. "Reagan's Moment: And America's?" *American Spectator* vol. 13, no. 7 (1980): 7–10.

Asher, Herbert B. *Presidential Elections and American Politics*. 4th ed. Chicago: Dorsey Press, 1988.

Barber, James David. *Choosing the President*. Englewood Cliffs, N.J.: Prentice Hall, 1974.

Barnds, William J. *The Right to Know, to Withhold, and to Lie*. New York: The Council on Religion and International Affairs, 1969.

Barrett, Lawrence. *Gambling With History*. New York: Penguin Books, 1984.

Berkman, Ronald, and Kitch, Laura W. *Politics in the Media Age*. New York: McGraw Hill, 1986.

Black, Edwin. *Rhetorical Criticism: A Study in Method*. Madison: University of Wisconsin Press, 1978.

Bonafede, Dom. "Scandal Time." *National Journal* vol. 19 (January 24, 1987): 199–200, 205–7.

Borelli, Stephen A. "Change in Presidential Appeals: The Case of Aid to the Contras." Paper read at the Annual Meeting of the Southern Political Science Association, Atlanta, Ga., 1988.

Borman, Ernest G. "A Fantasy Theme Analysis of the Television Coverage of the Hostage Release and the Reagan Inaugural." *Quarterly Journal of Speech* vol. 62, no. 2 (1982): 133–45.

Burnham, Walter Dean. *The Current Crisis in American Politics*. New York: Oxford University Press, 1982.

Campbell, Karlyn Kohrs. *Critiques of Contemporary Rhetoric*. Belmont: Wadsworth Publishing, 1972.

Cannon, Lou. "Media Chose Wrong Target in Hitting Subordinates for Blackout." *Washington Post*, November 7, 1983, p. A3.

———. *Reagan*. New York: G. P. Putnam's Sons, 1982.

Cohen, Richard. "Hey!" *Washington Post*, November 13, 1983, p. B1.

Cronin, Thomas E. *The State of the Presidency*. Boston: Little, Brown, and Co., 1975.

Dalleck, Robert. *Ronald Reagan: The Politics of Symbolism*. Cambridge, Mass.: Harvard University Press, 1984.

Davis, James W. *The American Presidency: A New Perspective*. New York: Harper and Row, 1987.

Davis, Vincent, ed. *The Post-Imperial Presidency*. New York: Praeger, 1980.

Denton, Robert E., and Hahn, Dan F. *Presidential Communication: Description and Analysis*. New York: Praeger, 1986.

Deutsch, Karl W. *The Nerves of Government: Models of Political Communication and Control*. New York: The Free Press, 1963.

Donaldson, Sam. *Hold On, Mr. President!* New York: Fawcett Crest, 1987.

Edelman, Murray. "Myths, Metaphors, and Political Conformity." *Psychiatry* vol. 30 (1967): 217–28.

Edwards, George C., III. *The Public Presidency: The Pursuit of Popular Support*. New York: St. Martin's Press, 1983.

Elder, Charles D., and Cobb, Roger W. *The Political Uses of Symbols*. New York: Longman, 1983.

Erickson, Paul D. *Reagan Speaks: The Making of an American Myth*. New York: New York University Press, 1985.

Fisher, Walter R., "Rhetorical Fiction and the Presidency." *Quarterly Journal of Speech* vol. 66, no. 2 (1980): 119–26.

Goethals, Gregor. "Religious Communication and Popular Piety." *Journal of Communications* vol. 35, no. 1 (1985): 149–56.

Green, David. *Shaping Political Consciousness: The Language of Politics in America from McKinley to Reagan*. Ithaca: Cornell University Press, 1987.

Green, Mark, and McColl, Gail. *There He Goes Again: Ronald Reagan's Reign of Error*. New York: Pantheon, 1983.

Greenstein, Fred I., ed. *Leadership in the Modern Presidency*. Cambridge, Mass.: Harvard University Press, 1988.

———. *The Reagan Presidency: An Early Assessment*. Baltimore: Johns Hopkins University Press, 1983.

Grossman, Michael Baruch, and Kumar, Martha Joynt. "The Limits of Persuasion: Political Communications in the Reagan and Carter Administrations." Paper read at the Annual Meeting of the American Political Science Association, Chicago, Ill., 1987.

———. "The Media as Insider and Adversary: The Subtext of White House Reporting During the Carter and Reagan Administrations." Paper read at the Annual Meeting of the Midwest Political Science Association, Chicago, Ill., 1987.

Hart, Roderick P. *The Sound of Leadership: Presidential Communication in the Modern Age*. Chicago: University of Chicago Press, 1987.

———. *Verbal Style and the Presidency: A Computer-Based Analysis*. Orlando, Fla.: Academic Press, 1984.

Heclo, Hugh, and Salamon, Lester M., eds. *The Illusion of Presidential Government*. Boulder: Westview, 1981.

Henry, William A., III. *Visions of America: How We Saw the 1984 Election*. Boston, New York: Atlantic Monthly Press, 1985.

Hiebert, Ray Eldon, and Spitzer, Carlton. *The Voice of Government*. New York: John Wiley and Sons, 1965.

Hofstadter, Richard. *The Paranoid Style in American Politics and Other Essays*. New York: Alfred A. Knopf, 1978.

James, Dorothy B. "Television and the Syntax of Presidential Leadership." *Presidential Studies Quarterly* vol. 18, no. 4 (1988): 737–39.

Jones, Charles O., ed. *The Reagan Legacy: Promise and Performance*. Chatham, N.J.: Chatham House, 1988.

Karp, Walter. "Liberty under Siege: The Reagan Administration's Taste for Autocracy." *Harper's*, November, 1985, pp. 53–67.

Kernell, Samuel. *Going Public: New Strategies of Presidential Leadership*. Washington, D.C.: CQ Press, 1986.

Klapp, Orrin. *Symbolic Leaders*. Chicago: Aldine Publishing Co., 1964.

Krasner, Michael. "Reagan's Manipulated Mandate." *Social Policy* vol. 11, no. 5 (1981): 26–28.

Kymlicka, B. B., and Matthews, Jean V. *The Reagan Revolution?* Chicago: Dorsey, 1988.

Lasswell, Harold, et al. *The Language of Politics: Studies in Quantitative Semantics*. New York: George W. Stewart, Inc., 1949.

Lewis, Anthony. "The Reasons for Lying." New York *Times*, October 13, 1986, p. A19.

Linsky, Martin. *Impact: How the Press Affects Policy*. New York: W. W. Norton, 1986.

Martin, Howard H. "President Reagan's Return to Radio." *Journalism Quarterly* vol. 61, no. 4 (1984): 817–21.

Merrelman, Richard M. "The Dramaturgy of Politics." *Sociological Quarterly* vol. 10 (1969): 216–41.

Mickleson, Sig. *The Electric Mirror: Politics in the Age of Television*. New York: Dodd and Mead, 1972.

Middleton, Drew. "Barring Reporters From the Battlefield." New York *Times Magazine*, February 5, 1984, p. 37.

Miller, James Nathan. "Ronald Reagan and the Techniques of Deception." *Atlantic Monthly*, February 1984, p. 62–68.

Moen, Matthew C. "The Political Agenda of Ronald Reagan: A Content Analysis of the State of the Union Messages." *Presidential Studies Quarterly* vol. 18, no. 4 (1988): 775–85.

Morgan, David. *The Capital Press Corps: Newsmen and the Governing of New York State*. Westport, Conn.: Greenwood Press, 1978.

Nesmith, Bruce. "Ronald Reagan, the Presidency, and White Evangelicals." Paper read at the Annual Meeting of the Southern Political Science Association, Atlanta, Ga., 1988.

Nichols, Marie Hochsmith. *Rhetoric and Criticism*. Baton Rouge, La.: LSU Press, 1963.

Nimmo, Dan. *Newsgathering in Washington: A Study in Political Communication*. New York: Atherton Press, 1962.

Novak, Michael. *Choosing Our King: Powerful Symbols in American Politics*. New York: Macmillan, 1974.

O'Neill, Thomas P. with Novak, William. *Man of the House: The Life and Political Memoirs of Speaker Tip O'Neill*. New York: Random House, 1987.

Orman, John M. *Presidential Secrecy and Deception: Beyond the Power to Persuade*. Westport, Conn.: Greenwood, 1980.

———. "Reagan's Imperial Presidency." Paper read at the Annual Meeting of the American Political Science Association, Chicago, Ill., 1987.

Orwell, George. "Politics and the English Language." In *The Orwell Reader*, edited by George Orwell. New York: Harcourt, Brace, and World, Inc., 1956.

Page, Benjamin I. *Choices and Echoes in Presidential Elections*. Chicago: University of Chicago Press, 1978.

Palmer, John L. and Sawhill, Isabel V., eds. *The Reagan Experiment: An Examination of Economic and Social Policies under the Reagan Administration*. Washington, D.C.: The Urban Institute, 1982.

Pfiffner, James P., and Hoxie, R. Gordon, eds. *The Presidency in Transition*. New York: Center for the Study of the Presidency, 1989.

Pollard, James E. *The Presidents and the Press*. New York: Octagon Books, 1973.

Reston, James. "How to Fool the People: Reagan's No-Fault Politics." New York *Times*, October 5, 1986, p. E6.

Ricoeur, Paul. "The Model of the Text." In *Interpretive Social Science*, edited by Paul Rabinow and Michael Sullivan. Berkeley: University of California Press, 1979.

Rivers, William L. *The Other Government: Power and the Washington Media*. New York: Universe Books, 1982.

Rodgers, Daniel T. *Contested Truths: Keywords in American Politics Since Independence*. New York: Basic Books, 1987.

Rogin, Michael Paul. *Ronald Reagan, the Movie: and Other Episodes in Political Demonology*. Berkeley: University of California Press, 1987.

Rowland, Robert C., and Payne, Roger A. "The Context-Embeddedness of Political Discourse: a Re-evaluation of Reagan's Rhetoric in the 1982 Midterm Election Campaign." *Presidential Studies Quarterly* vol. 14, no. 2 (1984): 500–11.

Rubin, Richard L. *Press, Party, and the Presidency*. New York: W. W. Norton, 1981.

Shannon, Wayne W. "Mr. Reagan Goes to Washington: Teaching Exceptional America." *Public Opinion* vol. 4 (December/January 1982): 13–17.

Shefter, Martin, and Ginsberg, Benjamin. "Institutionalizing the Reagan Regime." Paper read at the Annual Meeting of the American Political Science Association, New Orleans, La., 1985.

Smith, Craig Allen. "Trouble Came to MisteReagan's Neighborhood: Observations on Iran/Contra and the Reagan Rhetoric." Paper read at the Annual Meeting of the American Political Science Association, Washington, D.C., 1988.

Smith, David, and Gebble, Melinda. *Reagan for Beginners*. London: Writers and Readers Publishing Co., 1984.

Smith, Hedrick, et al. *Reagan: The Man, the President*. New York: Macmillan, 1980.

Smith, William R. *The Rhetoric of American Politics*. Westport, Conn.: Greenwood, 1969.

Sorauf, Frank J. *Party Politics in America*. Boston: Little, Brown, 1984.

Speakes, Larry, with Pack, Robert. *Speaking Out: Inside the Reagan White House*. New York: Charles Scribner's Sons, 1988.

Stockman, David A. *The Triumph of Politics: How the Reagan Revolution Failed*. New York: Harper and Row, 1986.

Stuckey, Mary E. *Getting into the Game: The Pre-Presidential Rhetoric of Ronald Reagan*. New York: Praeger, 1989.

Tebbel, John, and Watts, Sarah Miles. *The Press and the Presidency: From George Washington to Ronald Reagan*. New York, Oxford: Oxford University Press, 1985.

Thomas, Helen. *Dateline: White House*. New York: Macmillan, 1975.

Thomas, Norman C. "The Presidency and Critical Scholarship in Perspective." Paper presented at the Annual Meeting of the American Political Science Association, New Orleans, La., 1985.

Thompson, Kenneth W., ed. *Ten Presidents and the Press*. Washington, D.C.: University Press of America, 1980.

———. *The White House Press on the Presidency*. Latham: University Press of America, 1983.

Walcott, Charles, and Hult, Karen M. "The Presidential Speechwriting Process: Evolution of an Organizational Function." Paper read at the Annual Meeting of the American Political Science Association, Washington, D.C., 1988.

Wayne, Stephen J. *The Road to the White House*. 3d ed. New York: St. Martin's Press, 1988.

White, James Boyd. *When Words Lose Their Meaning: Constitutions and Reconstitutions of Language, Character, and Community*. Chicago: University of Chicago Press, 1984.

Will, George F., ed. *Press, Politics, and Popular Government*. Washington, D.C.: The American Enterprise Institute, 1972.

Wills, Garry. *Reagan's America: Innocents at Home*. Garden City, N.Y.: Doubleday, 1985.

Windt, Theodore Otto, Jr. "Presidential Rhetoric: Definition of a Field of Study." *Presidential Studies Quarterly* vol. 16, no. 1 (1986): 102–6.

Windt, Theodore Otto, Jr., and Ingold, Beth, eds. *Essays in Presidential Rhetoric*. Dubuque: Kendall/Hunt, 1983.

Index

ABOUT THE AUTHOR

MARY E. STUCKEY is an Assistant Professor at the University of Mississippi, where she teaches courses on the U.S. presidency and political communication. She received her doctorate from the University of Notre Dame in 1987. She is the author of *Getting Into the Game: The Pre-Presidential Rhetoric of Ronald Reagan,* and numerous papers on the presidency and presidential rhetoric.